I SMELL SMOKE

BY

BILL R. THOMAS

COPYRIGHT © BY BILL R. THOMAS

ALL RIGHTS RESERVE

PRINTED IN THE UNITED STATES OF AMERICA

TO FRANK DULL, JIM FRANCIS, AND GENE ROSSELOT
(MY B-47 FELLOW CREW MEMBERS)

Thanks guys for a memorable experience - and Thank God
we won without having to drop a hydrogen bomb.

INTRODUCTION

This is a true story about a short time frame in the cold war. It is factual but written from my memory - certain names have been changed to protect the survivors. I freely confess that I have not done any significant research in writing this book, so, some of the technician stuff might be off just a tad.

It is also the story of the Strategic Air Command (SAC) and a B-47 aircraft crew - from their early training to the final breakup of the crew when I returned to civilian life. Enjoy.

Bill Thomas

TABLE OF CONTENTS

Chapter		Page
1	A Day Over The Arctic	1
2	Massive Retaliation	4
3	Tit For Tat	8
4	The B-47 Stratojet	11
5	How I got Into SAC	16
6	Flying and Navigation	25
7	The First Fatality	31
8	Bomb(s) Away	36
9	Assignment - 45th BS, 40th BW - Smoky Hill AFB, Kansas	41
10	Transition To The B-47	45
11	Finally - Combat Ready	48
12	Steve Canyon - Not	53
13	Survival Training - SAC Style	57
14	That Night in Reno	77
15	Target Assigned	79
16	Alert!	82
17	Everything Was Normal - The Smoke Was Black and The Flame Was Red	85

TABLE OF CONTENTS

Chapter		Page
18	Rotation	93
19	Anyone For Bridge	106
20	Skip Bought The Farm	108
21	Off Duty in Europe	111
22	Tired of Being Folked About	120
23	Return to Kansas	131
24	Hunting and Fishing In Kansas	133
25	Sad Day at Smoky Hill	137
26	Adios S.A.C. - Hello Texas	139

CHAPTER 1

A DAY OVER THE ARCTIC

It was a beautiful October day - the sky was so clear you could see forever. The air was cold and crisp and the contrails billowing from the six jet engines from the three B-47 Stratojets left huge tracks behind us in the clear arctic sky. We were the lead aircraft in the formation which was nearing the North Pole. Captain Jones and his crew were on our left wing and Captain Houser and his crew were on our right wing. Major Frank Dull, our aircraft commander, came on the intercom and said Jim, those guys are crowding us too close - I can't even make a turn - how far is Jones from our wing tip? Jim looked around and studied the situation for a minute before replying "he's tucked in closer than the blue angels - maybe ten feet". Frank said "this is dangerous - I'll cure this problem quickly". He switched from intercom to our in flight communications frequency and said "I Smell Smoke".

That broke up the tight formation immediately as Jones peeled left and Houser right. Everyone started talking at once I don't see anything - I don't smell smoke, etc., etc. However, they kept a respectable distance from us for rest of the flight and we crossed the North Pole and did a 180 (180 degree turn) and headed back to home base at Smoky Hill AFB, Salina, Kansas.

Why did the aircraft scatter like quail and the possibility of fire? Quite simply because each aircraft place was a flying fuel cell. A tiny spark in the wrong place could cause one helluva explosion.

We (SAC-B47's with hydrogen bombs) were the most powerful and potentially the most destructive force on the planet earth at that time. We were combat ready crews of the Strategic Air Command in the mid 50's - each aircraft could carry a hydrogen bomb in the bomb bay and each bomb was capable of destroying a major city and everything in it - anywhere on earth. The flight over the arctic was merely one of our routine flying requirements. It really wasn't that routine however, because the only tool you had available to navigate the arctic regions in those days was the gyroscope. The magnetic compass was worthless and there were no radio beacons up there on the ice cap and of course - no satellite G.P.S. and - gyros sometimes "tumbled". Thus, crews who flew up there the first time had a tendency to stay close to the leader.

The B-47 Stratojet bomber had ushered in the jet age for the Strategic Air Command and provided the United States with a quick and massive strike nuclear deterrent to anyone, anywhere - particularly Russia. This was the height of the cold war and we were quite capable of destroying Russia at the time - and they knew it.

General Curtis Lemay had taken command of the Strategic Air Force in 1947 and had built it into probably the most powerful and deadliest war machine of all time. He spent millions (if not billions) of taxpayer dollars building this fighting force which ultimately won the cold war against the communist - without ever dropping a bomb or firing a shot.

It is amazing how little the average U.S. Citizen knows about the "Cold War." It was a game of wits, technology, money and people. Had our national leadership faltered during those days - we could have lost the war to the communist. They had some good stuff too.

CHAPTER 2

MASSIVE RETALIATION

What was the "Cold War" all about? When did it start? How did we get into the position we were in - in the late 1950's? What was the political and military strategy? Massive nuclear retaliation you say - what the heck is that?

Bear in mind that this writer is a simple country boy that got swept up into this high level chess game and the explanations that follow are simple explanations to very complex questions. They are based solely upon personal observations and experiences and a fading memory and almost no research. If you are looking for a lot of philosophical and/or technical bull crap - you won't find it in this story.

The cold War was merely an extension of the big war that started when life began on Planet Earth. It is probable that the first two living things on the planet, whatever they were, fought for something - survival - food, shelter, whatever? That's just the way it is - we fight over stuff.

Mankind probably started fighting with what was available - fists, feet. Then, someone who was not doing so well with fist and feet probably picked up a stick or limb and used it as a club. Next, the feller who was getting clubbed to death might have reached down and picked up a big rock and threw it at the Wielder of the club. And before you knew it - others joined in and you had groups fighting groups. And from that beginning, weapons of war and strategies and tactics of war began to evolve. Improvements in weapons of war went through bows and arrows, spears, lances, catapults, then the metals - swords, mail, etc., and next gunpowder followed by guns of all sorts and sizes followed by tanks, aircraft, ships, etc., etc. Get the picture?

Every time new technology was advanced we came up with weapons that would kill more folks and more often; counter measures were developed which would negate or adversely affect the weapons developed. Probably the last good war on planet Earth was World War II. Our weapons had not advanced to the point that a human (be it soldier, sailor, airman, marine) was not important and could have a significant effect on the outcome of certain skirmishes or battles - in other words, there was still a place for human heroics and hero's.

The atomic bomb was invented during the closing stages of World War II. the dropping of the A-bombs on Nagasaki and Hiroshima, Japan have been credited, by historians, with shortening World War II and therefore saving many human lives. (The Japanese might take exception with this conclusion).

In my opinion, the invention of the atomic bomb was one of a handful of events in history that completely changed the course of <u>future</u> events. I think the a-bomb created a belief by mankind that the human race could be and might be someday destroyed. This belief became subliminal and led to the completely pleasure seeking and materialistic motives form the 60's forward and the almost complete erosion of morals and moral values.

Sorry - I sometimes digress and start preaching. Back to "massive retaliation."

With the amount of nuclear weapons in our possession after World War II. the U.S. basically told the USSR - "If you start a war folks - we will retaliate with enough nuclear weapons to <u>completely</u> destroy you."

The ability to carry out this threat became the charge of the <u>Strategic Air Command</u> (SAC). SAC was commanded by General Curtis Lemay who was both revered and feared by all the flight crews under his command. Regardless of what you thought or think about the man, you must give him credit for getting the job done. There is no doubt in my mind that, had a nuclear war started in the late 50's the USSR would have been <u>destroyed</u>!

Here is the way the SAC massive retaliation concept was designed (the "game plan"); it is relatively simple. All of our rigid training was designed to assure that we would successfully carry out his "Game Plan." In those days, S.A.C. crews were comprised basically of World War II pilots, flight school graduates, and college graduate R.O.T.C. officers.

Many times I remembered the cracker barrel philosophy of my granddad - Lib Thomas. He always said the best way to get along with folks was to get along with folks was to be stronger, meaner, and tougher than everyone else and never take any crap off anybody. He always concluded with the observation - when a big tough dog walks up to other dogs - you never see any little dogs jump on him - do you? Nope - never did.

CHAPTER 3

TIT FOR TAT

Since we (the good ole U.S.A.) were equipped and ready to destroy the bad guys (bad ole USS) I suspect they were fully aware of our plans. Does it not stand to reason that if they planned to attack us it would have been a <u>massive</u> attack designed to completely destroy us? When you stop to really think about the cold war - <u>it's</u> <u>scary</u> <u>as</u> <u>all</u> <u>get</u> <u>out</u>.

And of course the weapons of war were not limited to the warplanes of the Strategic Air Command. The navy had its ships, planes, and submarines and the army it's men, tanks, and guns, and the marines - their marines and shining swords. But prior to the refinement of the missiles, the primary responsibility for delivery of nuclear weapons rested with S.A.C. and it's long-range bombers.

This was a relatively short time span that SAC bombers reigned supreme - they were replaced in the 1960's by the Intercontinental Ballistic Missiles (ICBM's). And the ICBM's were hopefully replaced by peace with the economic collapse of Russia in the 1980's. They simply went bankrupt before we did.

However, back to the heyday of the long range bombers. Remember, I told you that the development of weapons was a game of point - counter point. Whenever one side develops a weapon for war - the other side tries to develop a weapon to counter it. This is an area where the spy's become extremely important - they steal each other's secrets.

The job of stopping the Russian bombers if they ever decided to attach us was in the hands of the Air Defense Command. They had high performance fighter planes (called interceptions) which would take off from their bases, climb high rapidly, find the bombers, and shoot them down. Later they used ground to air missiles.

A line of radar installations (called the dew line) stretched across Canada to give them "Early" warning that the Russians were on their way. (Assuming they came across the Arctic of course). That job is now handled by orbiting spy satellites. Here again, we can assume the Russians had similar capabilities.

In actuality, it took time to development all this stuff and at any point in time - one side or the other had an advantage -All be it sometimes slight. I remember in my earlier days of combat

training as part of a B-47 crew, we were required to get so many intercepts by Air Defense Command Fighters. This was in the days they had F-84, F-86, and F-89's. We had to call ahead and give them 15 or 20 minutes notice of where we would meet them to give them ample time to get to altitude and meet us. And once they started an intercept, all we had to do was turn to evade them. The stalled and fell out of the sky, but the time the F-94's came along - the positions reversed.

CHAPTER 4

THE B-47 STRATOJET

All aircraft go through certain modifications during their service lives - especially military aircraft. The B-47 was no exception. From a flight crew point of view - it seemed like they were constantly modifying our airplane. The factory reps lived with us. We made several trips ferrying the aircraft back to the factory for major modifications. And we also spent many hours in school - learning how to use the new equipment.

As I recall, the history of the B-47 Stratojet was somewhat as follows: The original design competition was between the following-

Manufactured	Type	No. of Engines	Wingspan	Top Speed
Boeing	B-47	6	116'	630
North American	B-45	4	96'	580
Convair	XB-46	4	113'	545
Martin	XB-48	6	108'	495

Boeing won and as soon as funding was available, the plane was literally thrown into production. New ground was being plowed with regand to the technology. Some of the major modifications after the aircraft was in service included:

*Installation of a fire control system for the twin 5o caliber machine guns mounted in the tail cone.

*Installation of ejection seats.

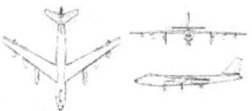

*Increased fuel capacity and structural strengthening.

*Replaced the J-47-GE23 engines with J47-GE25 engines and addition of a water alcohol injection system.

*Increased bomb bay capacity.

*Addition of Phase III ECM (Electronic Counter Measures).

*Addition of A-LARC-21X long range liaison radio

*Addition of approach chute.

The B-47 had been rushed into service to meet the needs of the U.S.A.F. During that particular time of the "Cold War". Another aircraft, the B-52, was being developed and the B-47 was an interim bomber until the B-52 was placed into service - about 2000 B-47's were built at a cost of approximately $18 mil (today's collars) each.

Despite its size - 110' long, 28' high, and 116' wingspan - gross weight 185,000 pounds - the B-47 had a crew of only 3 - pilot (aircraft commander), co-pilot, and observer (navigator - bombardier), the initial crews were cross trained in each position - the theory being that if one member became incapacitated in flight, another member could take his place during a critical time. For example, if the observer became stricken on a bomb run - the co-pilot could complete the run and drop the bomb. Or, if the pilot became stricken on a landing, the co-pilot could take his place and the observer take the co-pilots place to safely land the aircraft. Some of the things that I remember about the constant changes that were taking place with the aircraft include the following:

One day we flew our aircraft to the Martin-Marietta plant in Marietta, Georgia from our base (Smokey Hills AFB, Salina, Kansas) for an Iran (inspect and repair as necessary) inspection. Everything was fine until we landed - then things began to get right sporty. There was a big hump about half way down the runway at Marietta. If you weren't familiar with it, the hump was so bad that the aircraft would literally become airborne again as it went over the hump. (It was a sort of standard joke with the locals). Sure enough, we landed a little bit long and hot - hit the hump - and became airborne again. Frank immediately shoved the throttle forward and we finished a "touch and go" and flew around to try it again. He wasn't satisfied on the next pass - nor the next and we attracted the attention of the locals in the tower. One of them said on his open mike "Guess we had better drag out the anti aircraft gun boys, the only way we're going to get these boys on the ground is to shout em down." We landed on the next pass.

CHAPTER 5

HOW I GOT INTO S.A.C.

I always remembered how Will was so impressed with Ben in <u>NO</u> <u>TIME</u> <u>FOR</u> <u>SERGEANTS</u> – cause Ben "had R.O.T.C."

I signed up for Air Force ROTC while attending the University of Kentucky – primarily because they paid you about $40 a month as I recall. The classes were easy and so was the marching. I had been walking and hiking all my life so a little ole 5 mile march was nothing.

I selected the Air Force because I had always wanted to fly – like a bird.

When I graduated from college they told us to not make any long-range plans – cause we would be called to active duty very soon. The Korean War had broken out – big time. Graduation was in June and I took a job with a national accounting firm in Cincinnati, Ohio. However, just before Christmas I received my orders to report to Lackland AFB, San Antonio, Texas on December 29th (1953).

When I left Cincinnati in my new mercury on the 27th there was over a foot of snow on the ground and it was very cold. I was dressed in warm wool clothes.

I entered Texas at a small town named Waskom – on the Louisiana border. It was early in the morning and I was hungry so I stopped there at a truck stop café and had breakfast. Two things convinced me I had stumbled into heaven – one, it was about 75 degrees and everyone was in short sleeves, and two – the breakfast menu had steak and eggs on it for a couple of dollars.

By late afternoon I had arrived in San Antonio. A close friend of mine, Tom Hopkins, was a year ahead of me in school and had been in the Air Force for about a year (another ROTC deal). He was stationed at Kelly AFB in San Antonio and we had kept in touch. He told me to call him when I got to San Antonio – so I did.

When I called Tom he instructed me to sit tight – he would drive over and lead me to their apartment. I waited and in a few minutes Tom and Annette, his wife, drove up. (Annette had been a friend in college also and I had introduced them.) Annette gave me a big hug and kiss and Tom nearly broke my hand with his handshake. They were both grinning when they told me they had a surprise waiting for me at their apartment.

I followed them home and when we parked and went inside – there stood the most gorgeous female of the species I had ever laid eyes on. She was a Mexican beauty named Carolina Nieto who taught school with Annette. We hit it off right from the start and by July we were married – still are.

That evening we went on a whirlwind tour of San Antonio (Alamo, River Walk, Mi Tierra, etc.) – then ate out at a steak house (think it was called the Red Barn).

By the time I was getting ready for bed at Tom's guest room, I had made two major decisions –

(1)   I was going to marry Carolina Nieto, and

(2)   Texas was going to be my adopted home for the rest of my life.

The next morning I was awakened by Tom and Annette as they were scurrying around – getting ready for work. I got up, grabbed a donut and a cup of coffee and awaited my turn in the bathroom to shave and get dressed. When they departed for work I departed for Lackland AFB (using a map that Tom had drawn for me). I had no difficulty locating Lackland and very soon I was being processing for active duty in the U.S. Air Force. This involved completing what seemed to be hundreds of forms, a complete physical exam, etc., etc. During the processing received and I received my BOQ (Bachelor Officers Quarters) assessment and some money – (travel, uniform account, etc.). It was near dark before I finally checked into my room and unloaded my stuff. I got directions to the mess hall from the airman at the front desk and after a light supper – I hit the hay – officially on active duty.

The next day was more leisurely – I went to the base exchange and bought some uniforms and shoes, got a haircut, cashed my travel check, and called Carolina. She accepted my invitation to dinner and a movie – and offered to drive (which I immediately accepted). Our first date was great. I was completely in awe of her beauty as well as her Spanish accent.

The next couple of days I attended some orientation meetings but otherwise loafed. There was a steady stream of new arrivals in the BOQ. (They were all ROTC grads – like me). We were told that we would begin formal training the following Monday. Carolina (Caro) and I had a date every night and the next weekend Tom and Annette joined us on a trip to Bandera, Texas. Bandera was the home of several dude ranches, bars, dance halls, etc. – it was a fun place (at least on this trip – a later trip was a little more sporty).

Monday morning we got organized real quick and started the Air Force version of "basic training" for officers. We had classroom lectures, P.E., marching, obstacle courses, etc. One thing I remember about our marching - the song we sang - up in the air junior birdmen, up in the air upside down, up in the air junior birdmen, don't ever let you feet touch the ground. I think this went on for around 4 weeks – about the end of the third week they had counseling sessions with us to find out what we wanted to be in the USAF. I suspect that at first, about 99% of us wanted to be pilots – particularly <u>fighter</u> <u>pilots</u>. We were warned that the Air Force had Quotas to fill that determined how many were sent to flight training. And there was one other factor – your duty was extended one year if you flew.

I was really lucky to have Tom as a friend. He gave me some additional counseling and advice. He strongly suggested that if I really wanted to fly, I should volunteer for multi engines and volunteer immediately for the Strategic

Air Command. My official counselor said it was too early in my career to volunteer for any particular command – however, Tom had spoken to him on my behalf and he did make note of my interest in S.A.C. and it stayed in my records.

Friday of that week was set aside for physical exams – and that "black" Friday will forever stay deeply imbedded in my mind. It changed my career plans drastically. When I took the eye examination, the doctor wrote something on my record but I didn't think much of it – my vision had always been 20/20. Later in the day my name was called and I stepped forward. They took me back to the eye examination room. This time they re-checked my eyes and gave me some further tests, finally the doctor said, "Lieutenant, I hate to be the one to tell you this – your left eye is only 20/30 and you don't qualify for flying training" I was devastated – surely they had made a mistake – this couldn't happen to me." I felt like crying.

A major (forgot his last name) took me into a private office and explained an alternative to becoming a pilot. He said the Strategic Air Command had a huge demand for aircraft observers for a new aircraft – the B-47. There were only three crew members on the B-47 – the pilot, co-pilot, and observer. The observer did all the navigator and bombing. He also was awarded wings and drew full flight pay. In many respects, it was more demanding than a pilots duties.

Since my choice now narrowed down to observer (flying) or a desk job (accounting) – I naturally chose observer.

The following Monday, the school assignments were posted on our bulletin board. Less than half of us (we must have totaled around two hundred) were scheduled for flight training at either Hondo AFB (Texas) or Sedalia AFB (MO.) – The balance of the class was going to "administrative" type schools, except for me and a few others who were assigned to aircraft observer training, Waco, Texas.

There was a two week delay between our basic training and my reporting date at James Connally AFB, Waco, Texas. I asked the training commander if there was "anything" I could do during those two weeks – he assigned me as a "mess officer.".

I went to the main mess hall about 9:00 a.m. the next morning. The mess sergeant and a couple of his assistants were sitting at a table drinking coffee. There were several airmen working at various tasks – mopping floors, washing dishes, etc. When I stepped through the door some young airmen saw me and screamed at the top of his lungs – attention." I yelled back a few decibels lower – at ease! And walked over to the mess sergeant. He came to attention again and saluted. I returned his salute and stuck out my hand and said "I'm Bill Thomas and I've been assigned as mess officer – may I join you? The sergeant shook my hand and said, "I'm sergeant Lou Tenerillo – I got a copy of the orders this morning and we've been expecting you. The crew is trying to get this place cleaned up for your inspection. He said – we're ready for inspection. I said – aw heck sergeant, I don't need to inspect this place – it looks good to me.

The sergeant said, it's customary for the new mess officer to do an inspection when he takes over – the men who have worked their tails off getting this place ready will be disappointed if you don't make an inspection. I said – well – o.k., but I've never made an inspection before in my life – what do I do? The sergeant replied – "Just be yourself."

Sergeant Tenerillo announced "inspection" and the men took their assigned stations. I was thinking fast and decided I was not going to criticize anything unless it was obviously (even to me) screwed up.

Sergeant Tenerillo joined me and we started the inspection tour in the dining area. It was spotless and squeaky clean. I stopped and asked – "Who was responsible for cleaning this area?" A very meek and small (in statue) airman said, almost in a whisper, "I was sir." He was turning white and starting the tremble as I walked over to him. I took, his hand and shook it solidly and said "Congratulations, this is the cleanest dining room I've ever seen – I would not hesitate to eat a biscuit that fell on this floor. I relaxed my grip and put my arm around his shoulder and squeezed him. He was smiling ear to ear as we headed to the kitchen.

That was my first encounter with a raw recruit and I had no idea they were so fearful of officers – that's one thing they learned real good in basic training. I vowed I would always treat the enlisted men with respect and dignity – and never take advantage of my rank.

The inspection of the kitchen, stores, and office contained similar repeat scenes. I took every opportunity to brag on the men. The old sergeant sort of had a puzzled look on his face.

When we finished the inspection everyone went back to work and it sort of seems that things perked up a little. We rejoined the other two NCO's at the table in the dining room and got some coffee. I asked "How did it go sergeant?' He responded with a question "was this really the cleanest dining room you have ever seen? I said "I don't lie and didn't lie – this is the only dining room I've ever seen."

He said "What do you want to do next?" I said "nothing'. He said, you mean you don't want us to do nothing – you're the boss.

I said "Hold on there sergeant – let's get a few things straight." He looked quizzically at me and I asked, "How long have you been in the Air Force" – he replied "24 years) and I next asked "How many years have you been a mess sergeant and running mess halls" – he responded "about 10 years."

I said, sergeant, I graduated from college with degrees in accounting and geology and I grew up on a poor hillside farm in Kentucky, I know a little bit about bookkeeping, rocks, and hard times. I took ROTC in college and that gave me these second lieutenant bars. I've been on active duty 5 weeks and in a couple of weeks I'll be shipping out to flight school. They gave me this job just to keep me off the streets. I know absolutely nothing about a mess hall – and don't really want to know about them. You run this place like you always have – like it's supposed to be run. Look on me as your helper – if there is anything I can do to help you – just ask and you got it. Comprendo! (I was already starting to pick up a little Spanish).

The sergeant looked at the other two NCO's and said – I've run across hundreds of shave tail Lieutenants in my career – but Lieutenant Thomas here takes the cake. He's smart and will go far in this man's Air Force.

CHAPTER 6

FLYING AND NAVIGATING

After two weeks of basically loafing, I was ready for some action as I drove up highway 35 from San Antonio to Waco. When I arrived at James Connally AFB – I was somewhat disappointed. It was rather bleak looking.

I processed in and was given my BOQ assignment. Classes didn't start until the next day so I spent most of the day wandering around the base. I had on my uniform but was having trouble getting used to saluting. Every time I met an enlisted man he would salute me – I always returned salutes. My problem was, when I met a ranking officer, I couldn't remember to salute him – until I met this bird colonel in front of the BOQ. I said "Howdy" and started in the BOQ. He "braced" me and proceeded to chew my tail out. From then on – I remembered.

After I made the rounds and returned to the BOQ – it was like a bee hive of activity. About fifty shave tailed lieutenants (like me) had checked in. They were all flying airplanes with their hands – some climbing, some diving, some banking left and some right. I introduced myself to several of them – but couldn't remember any names. It got dark finally so I went to sleep.

Classes began promptly at 0800 the next day – ground school. I had always been an avid reader and had read everything I could get my hands on about flying, navigation, warfare (particularly aerial combat) and – weather.

I aced ground school – no problems at all. And really – no problems after we started flight training.

In the Air Force acronyms and clichés came fast and furious. It seemed the Air Force language was built around them. However, once you had them memorized – no sweat (see what I mean). And you never forget most of them – i.e. – there are old pilots and there are bold pilots – but there are no old, bold pilots." The name of the game in multi engines was strictly – <u>straight</u> and <u>level</u>. (No acrobatics and fancy stuff). I started thinking of myself as a greyhound bus driver. Crank that baby up and get where you are going – no horsing around – strictly business. The main difference in flying (other than the straight and level) was that with two engines – you had twice as many engine gages. However, you had twice as many pilots also – a pilot and a co-pilot. In many respects, the multi engines were easier to fly because it didn't have the engine Torque effect that you had in a single engine. Also, they were <u>alleged</u> to be safer – if one engine quit – you could remain airborne on the others.

After we completed ground school we did our flight training in a T-46 (similar to the old C-47) and later in a T-25 (converted B-25's). Our flights were longer and we converted much more territory – once we flew out to Bermuda on a navigator training flight. That was a real treat.

Each flight was a combination of flight training and navigation training. I rose to the top of my class – in <u>navigating</u>. It just came natural to me – again the logic. I could understand and visualize the effect the wind had on the aircraft over time and distance and that was what navigation was all about.

I became so proficient with the sextant that the instructor made me his assistant. I helped train my classmates.

We were supposed to get a couple of days off for the July 4th weekend so Caro and I decided we would take advantage of my days off to get married. I was driving to San Antonio every weekend to see her and would stay there until the last minute before returning to Waco. That almost got me killed. I owned a Mercury sedan that had a large V/8 engine and overdrive. It would "cruise" at about 110 mph. I left San Antonio one Monday morning about 4:00 a.m. and was scheduled to fly at 7:00 a.m.

The Mercury was flying low when I hit the curve at Round Rock. I think I had dozed off for I woke up about the time I left the pavement and crashed through some ranchers barbed wire fence – finally stopping out in the middle of the pasture. My car didn't turn over but I tore heck out of the front end – busted lights, punctured radiator, dents, scratches, and both front tires flat. I had knocked a couple of teeth loose and had a black eye – otherwise, no serious damage.

Of course, the highway patrol showed up, then a wrecker, ambulance, and one irate rancher. I gave the rancher what money I had to fix his fence and told him I d pay the balance if he would send me a bill. The ambulance left and the wrecker driver agreed to tow my car to the Round Rock Ford dealer to get it fixed. I gave him my address, phone number, and a Gulf credit card. He agreed to send me a bill and return my credit card when I paid him. He also agreed to have the Ford dealer call me about fixing my car.

But the nicest one of all turned out to be trooper Jackson of the Texas highway patrol. He had been in pilot training himself but had "washed out" and spent three years as an aircraft mechanic. When he found out who I was and what I did - he volunteered to drive me to Waco so I wouldn't get in trouble with the Air Force. I've never forgotten that man – God Bless him and his get.

With Trooper Jackson's help I made it back in time to make my flight. I talked to the Ford dealer that night and gave them my insurance information, etc. The next weekend I rode the bus to Round Rock and picked up my Mercury – it was good as new. The wrecker was paid and I got my Gulf card back – everything was fine – except I had to fly on July 4th. We postponed our wedding until July 7th – a Saturday. Caro came up to Waco a couple of days before and took care of all the arrangements – wedding, honeymoon, and apartment for later. Her sister was to be bridesmaid and my roommate, Bill Nesbit (from North Carolina) was best man.

Our wedding became a class project – everyone pitched in. It was to be a fast version of a military wedding and our honeymoon was a two day trip to Padre Island.

The next few days passed in a wink of the eye. The wedding weekend arrived. The first event was the bachelor party – which turned out to be a class "koolie howe" which was planned and implemented by a classmate, Jim Fitzgerald (Chicago).

It was held at the city park and was supposed to be Hawaiian style – roast pig, luaus, etc. It was mostly watermelons split open and saturated with vodka. There were a couple of photos made at that party that I've tried to obtain (and destroy) over the years – without success. In one, we are all gathered around the fire and I'm standing behind this topless female – my arms around her and my hands clasping her breast. (I'm sure I was just protecting them from the heat of the fire.)

We were so overhung the next day for the wedding that I hardly remember it – but there are about fifty witnesses that swear it took place. After the reception at the officers club we got into the Mercury and raced away to Padre Island – tin cans flying. I stopped at the first car wash and washed some of the smutty stuff off the car.

I don't remember Padre either – not even sure I saw it that trip. I think we just checked into a hotel and spent the next two days in bed. Then we raced back to our apartment in Waco and I was back on Monday morning. A trip to the apartment for lunch S.O.P. (Standard Operating Procedure) the next couple of months.

My folks came down (from Kentucky) and Caro's folks came up from Presidio (Texas) for Labor Day weekend. It was the first time the two families had met – everything turned out just great.

CHAPTER 7

THE FIRST FATALITY

From day one in flight training we had been warned of the dangers of flying – over and over and over. They even told us that 6% of us would die in flight training. But of course, we were young and infallible and didn't believe it. We were are college graduates - too smart to crash an airplane. Invincible!

Two of my classmates and best friends and their wives lived in the apartments where we lived (Westway apartments – Waco). They were Grafton and Mary Smith from Atlanta, GA and Bob and Cindy Brown from Richmond, VA. We did a lot of things together – while we were in class or flying, or off duty.

Caro and I had not been married quite two months when it happened. It was a Wednesday night, the 2nd day of September. I had a horrible dream – I dreamed that Grafton was riding as navigator in a B-25 and it was in some terrible weather – really bouncing around. Then I saw fire coming out of the right engine. The plane went into a diving spiral. Smoke was also coming out of the left engines. I thought I was yelling "Grafton – Bail out! Bail out! Then I saw the spin tighten as the plane plummeted to Earth. Finally the trip ended in a huge fireball as it crashed into a plowed field. I awoke and sat up in bed and started to cry. Caro awoke, turned on a lamp, and said "Why are you awake – and crying – it's 3:00 o'clock in the morning." I looked at the clock – it was 3:04.

I told her "Grafton just got killed in a plane crash".

She said "How do you know that? Did someone call?" I said "No, I saw it happen in my dream". She said "You just had a nightmare – go back to sleep." I lay there in bed – trying to convince myself that it was just a dream and trying to get back to sleep – but could not.

I had been lying there about an hour when I heard a car drive into the apartment parking lot and saw the reflection of its lights and heard the car door slam. In a couple of minutes I heard a woman scream. This woke Caro a second time – she sat up and asked "Did you hear a scream?" I said "Yes" and jumped up and pulled on a pair of pants and slipped into my house slippers. I opened the door and stepped out – several lights were on throughout the apartments.

I could hear a woman crying loudly - it sounded like it was coming from the Smith's apartment. Caro had come to the door and commented "that sounds like Mary Jane (Smith) crying. I replied "I think it is – I'm going over to their apartment and find out." She said – "No – wait." Then she put on a rope, handed me a shirt which I slipped on – and we walked together to the Smith's apartment.

The door to their apartment was ajar and we had guessed right. Our training squadron commander, Lt. Col. Stapleton and a Chaplin, Lieutenant Moss, were inside the apartment – trying to comfort Mary Jane who was just bawling. She saw us standing in the door and shouted

"Grafton is dead."

I embraced her and she cried on my shoulder a while – then Caro took over. The Chaplin finally got her to take a sedative and finally she quit crying – at least so loudly. In a few minutes, Bob and Cindy (Brown) came in – and Mary Jane started bawling again. Col. Stapelton motioned for me to follow him and we stepped outside. He said that Lt. Brown and I were excused from classes and/or flying the next day and he requested that we do whatever we could to help Mary Jane. He gave me his phone number and asked that I call him if I need anything . I told him I would.

Then I said "Colonel, I know this is going to be difficult to believe but I had a dream last night and "saw" Grafton get killed." He asked "Would you mind telling me about your dream?" I described by dream in detail, including the time I woke up – 3:04 a.m. He starred at me in amazement. He said "Lieutenant, this is absolutely amazing – I think you did experience something super natural. Would you mind telling this story to the people who will be investigating this clash? I said that I would be glad to he p. He said they would come by the next day to talk to me.

Colonel Stapleton said that the information he had was that the B-25 had completed the training flight and the pilot, Capt. Bob Powell, had called the tower and said he was 25 miles north of the base and requested a direct approach landing. He said they were in severe weather and running short on fuel. The tower picked them up on radar and gave them landing instructions. Capt. Powers called back in about two minutes and reported an emergency – said the plane had been struck by lighting and one engine was on fire and he was losing power in the other one. He said the canopy was stuck and he couldn't open to bail out. Then, they disappeared from radar. Emergency vehicles were dispatched from the base immediately – they found the wreckage in a plowed field just outside the small town of Penelope. (about 12 miles north of the base.)

The next day was tough. We did our best to help Mary Jane in her time of need – but she remained distraught. The thing that really saved her was the fact she was pregnant. She kept saying – "I've got to get a hold of myself for Grafton's child sake." She decided to have the funeral and burial in Atlanta. I called Col. Stapleton and he took care of having the body sent there, etc.

My saddest assignment that day was talking to Grafton's parents. They called Mary Jane and I answered her phone. She finally talked to them briefly – but broke down and could talk no more. Late that afternoon, Mary Jane's parents arrived and took over. The sad day had finally ended.

The next day I was flying. I was having trouble concentrating until my instructor chewed me out. He said – "You're lucky this is just training and not combat – there you really find out what danger and death are all about". I think it was at the end of this flight that I truly understood what a successful flight and landing is all about – if you walk away safely and healthy – that's all that matters. (later in the huge B-47's – we didn't call them landing at all – they became "Controlled crashes."

Navigation was complete – bombing next.

CHAPTER 8

BOMB(S) AWAY

The next assignment was bombing and special weapons training at Mather AFB, Sacramento, California. Again, we had about ten (10) days before the next training class was scheduled to begin. We decided to drive from Waco to Sacramento. Since our route would take us through west Texas – we further decided to spend a few days with Caro's family in Presidio, Texas (the hottest place on earth - in the summer). We would be there over the Christmas holidays. Before we left we bought a new car – '55 Chevy Bel Air. We loaded our possessions (our clothes plus a T.V. set) and headed west. The trip to Presidio was uneventful and after sitting around Caro's house for a couple of days – I was getting very bored. Her father asked me "Do you like to hunt." I said "more than I like to eat when I'm hungry." He said "I'm going to my ranch tomorrow – be gone for about a week – want to come along?" I quickly accepted the invitation.

He had a general merchandise store in Presidio. His ranch was about 100 miles south - in the state of Chihuahua, Mexico. In those days – it was dirt road all the way. What an adventure this turned out to be – it was like going back 150 years in time – to the days of the early settlement of Texas. My father-in-law's ranch was over 200,000 acres and carried over 6,000 head of cattle. It was operated by Vaqueros on horseback. I spent a week out in the wilds with two of the Vaqueros – we rode horses and slept on the ground. This trip is covered in another book – <u>My Greatest Hunting Adventure</u> and <u>My Greatest Fishing Adventure</u>!

We almost didn't make it back to Presidio on time. It had rained and washed out a bridge and we got stuck in the mud a couple of times, even though the truck had 4 wheel drive. When we got to Presidio, I took a quick shower, shaved, got dressed, and jumped in the new Chevy. Caro had everything packed. We sped away toward California. We drove until late into the night but couldn't pass Las Vegas – we stopped there and got a room and then hit the "strip". We ended up back at our room as the sun was rising. We slept until noon then started west again.

This first thing we did when we arrived in Sacramento was purchase a newspaper and a city map. In short order we located an apartment and moved in – that is, unloaded the T.V. set and our clothes. I've always been a shy country boy but Caro is very gregarious. Within an hour she met Bill & Pedie West who lined a couple of doors down the hail from us. They were from Miami and Bill was Air Force – scheduled for bombing and special weapons school also. They had arrived the day before. Bill drove a bright red T-Bird – the first I ever rode in.

They both loved seafood and had located a great seafood restaurant about a mile from the apartment (Coral Gables Apts. As I remember). The four of us went to dinner that evening and got better acquainted. Bills dad was a general contractor in Miami and Bill described how his dad had buried old cars along the beach to expand the beach area before he constructed hotels, etc. Apparently he was quite wealthy.

The next day, I rode to Mather with Bill. We processed in and went to class. It was near the close of that first day of classes before I realized what "special weapons" were. Heck, we were going to be studying about <u>atomic</u> <u>bombs</u> and <u>hydrogen</u> <u>bombs</u> – scary stuff.

For the next several weeks we studied the bombs and how to deliver them to the target. Then we climbed into airplanes and started applying what we had learned. I think we "bombed" every town in California – from San Diego to Mendocino. We started with the old WWII Vintage Norden Bombsights and advantage to the latest radar controlled K-4 bombing system.

Not bragging – just fact. I was the best bombardier in my class. I quickly learned to use "Kentucky windage". My first bomb might be a little off target but the following bombs were usually bulls eye.

Perhaps I have deceived you about the bombing. We were not actually dropping bombs. We did everything in the air you would normally do to drop a bomb - line up on the I.P. (initial point) – point the aircraft on a heading toward the target – compute the "drop" time – adjust our wind calculation - locate the "target", place the + on the target and the plane on auto pilot, fly the plane to release point, turn on the camera and take pictures, hit the bomb release – and get ready for another bomb run.

A radar set on the ground tracked the airplane down the bomb run. It was hooked into a computer which determined (based on our altitude, speed, the wind, and theoretical "bomb",) the exact spot in space we should be at bomb release to hit the target. When we hit bomb release it sent an electronic signal to the computer – the computer then measured the distance and direction the plane was from theoretical release point. The ground station would then call us with the results (in code).

I was sworn to secrecy about the bombs so I guess I'd best not say much about them. (However, while we were in class, one of the students brought a POPULAR MECHANICS magazine to class which described the atomic bomb in greater detail than our textbooks - I think by now most everyone knows how to build an atomic bomb).

Bombing was fun – I really enjoyed this training and hated to see it come to a close. Northern California was a neat place in those days too – it was not overcrowded and was laid back. We might spend one weekend in San Francisco and the next in the Sierra Nevada – camping out and panning for gold. And Bill let me drive his T-Bird a few times – what a blast!

My next orders came – transition (to B-47) training at McConnell AFB, Wichita Kansas.

We dutifully loaded the TV set and headed back east. I had fallen in love with the pacific northwest and decided I wanted to move to Oregon (instead of Texas) when my tour of duty was complete. (bad mistake).

CHAPTER 9

ASSIGNMENT – 45TH BS, 40TH BW –

SMOKEY HILL AFB, KANSAS

Before we completed bombardier training and special weapons school our permanent duty station orders came in. I can't say that I was particularly thrilled with mine. I was assigned to the 45th bombardment squadron, 40th bomb wing, 8th Air Force, United States strategic Air Command located at Smokey Hill (later renamed to Shilling AFB) AFB, Salina, Kansas. I really became more disappointed when we started comparing assignments – particularly with classmates who were going to Florida (MacDill, Homestead, and Pinecastle); Indiana (Bunker Hill); Louisiana (Barksdale); Ohio (Lockbourne) New York (Plattsburg), New Hampshire (Pease); California (March and Castle), Texas (Dyess and Biggs), Arizona (Davis Monthan), and Idaho (Mountain Home). I would have gladly traded assignments with any of them – and given "Boot".

When we completed this training there was a graduation exercise in which we received our wings (observer). Of course, a big party and much celebration followed.

The next day we said farewell to our classmates and California and drove east toward Kansas. The trip through the Rockies was beautiful. Caro was a little bit pregnant and had both morning sickness and car sickness – but we finally made it to Salina and I processed in. I learned there was no Base Housing and darn few apartments available in Salina. It seemed most crew members owned or rented houses in an off base housing project on the west side of Salina called Indian Village.

We spent the next couple of days in Indian Village – looking for a place to live. It was summer and hot and dry – and I had a pregnant and irritable wife to contend with. Nothing we looked at pleased her – she found fault with everything. Finally, toward the end of the second day we found a two bedroom house on Cherokee St. with a "For sale by owner" sign in the yard. Caro liked it so we bought it. The owners (Ed and Sue Clark) still lived there but were building a new home a couple of blocks away and were going to move within a week. We decided another week in the Best Western Motel wouldn't be too bad – besides, it would give Caro time to buy furniture for our new home while I took care of Air Force matters. The sellers (who were native to Salina) sort of adopted us. I don't know how we would have made it without them.

I'm sure that everyone who has bounced around the U.S.A. in military service has had the same experience. Most of the people you meet, both in and out of the service, are good folks. They go out of their way to help you. It's really a great country and you realize that risking your life to defend it is really worth it.

My first week with the 45th was hectic. I met most of the crew members, the squadron commander (Col. Hempleman), the operations officer, (Major Zisk) and some of the enlisted support people. About the second day – Col. Hempleman called me into his office and introduced me to Capt. Frank Dull and Lt. Jim Francis. He handed us our orders assigning us as crew NR92 and gave us a little pep talk. He described that we would be next going to Wichita for B-47 transition training and when we returned we would continue "On the job" training – the end result being – classification as a "Combat ready" R – crew status.

Next, we were assigned lockers, flight suits, helmets, etc. and were ready to begin the adventure. We did a lot of coffee drinking and visiting the next couple of days. I learned that Frank had flown B-29's during World War II and was among the many pilots who had been recalled to active duty when the Korean war broke out (it was still raging at that time). He and his wife Kathryn were from Cleveland, Ohio – both were catholic and they naturally had a large family – 5 children. Frank had owned an air conditioning business in Cleveland and wasn't all that pleased to be back in the Air Force – but he was there and decided to give it his best shot. He was an excellent pilot and as it turned out – I was extremely fortunate to be crewed up with him. He was a cool customer under pressure and that fact saved our lives – more than once.

Jim Francis was a Kansas wheat farmer – fresh out of pilot training. He was very large – about 6'4" – 230 lbs. He and his wife Carol were the best friends you could have – salt of the earth. They both grew up on wheat farms near Wichita. Jim was also an excellent pilot.

That week passed fast. The Clarks had moved, Caro had spent our savings for new furniture, etc. and I was now heavily in debt to Sears Roebuck for appliances, etc. Fortunately, I had been promoted to first Lieutenant in June and was now on flight pay (extra $100 a month) so, all in all, we were in fair shape financially – and we had our first "home".

The next week we went to Wichita for B-47 transition. Since it was going to be a relatively short course we decided to commute. We took turns driving. Frank and Jim also lived in Indian Village – didn't everyone?

CHAPTER 10

TRANSITION TO THE B-47

I fell in love with the B-47 the first time we rolled down the runway, broke contact with mother earth, pulled the nose up and climbed skyward – my what power – you could feel it. The more I flew in the plane – the greater the love and respect for it. Folks, it was one heck of an aircraft – probably the Grand daddy of all of today's commercial airliners.

In Chapter 4, I described the history and evolution of the B-47. At McConnell we simply learned how to fly it. In many respects, it was easier to "drive" than the old B-25's had been in advanced – except for landings that is. The landing (stall) speed was 130 knots and the pilot and co-pilot seats were about 25 feet above the ground. Landings were truly 'controlled crashes".

In transition, we did basically the same things I had done it observer training and bombing training – we flew navigation legs and made numerous bomb runs – and the pilots (Frank and Jim) made jillions of touch and go landings and radar controlled landings. (I monitored all landings on my radar set). Since the planes were equipped with the same equipment I had trained on – that was no problem – the problem was the speed at which we traveled – about 600 mph – 3 times the speed of the training aircraft. It forced you to think fast and plan ahead – when you were covering 10 miles across mother earth every minute – it didn't take long for the plane to get way ahead of you if you weren't constantly alert. As each mission was completed, Frank, Jim, and I were becoming more and more confident with ourselves, each other, and the plane. We were developing into a real team. On long nav runs, Jim and I would swap seats – he would navigate and I would get to handle the controls. Each time I sat in the co-pilot seat – I damned my "weak" eye. Nevertheless, I was proud to at least be a crew member and knew that the success of most missions rested on my shoulders far more than the shoulders of the pilots. I resolved to become one of the very best observers is S.A.C.

The instructors who flew with us were grading us on every flight. We didn't know that at the time. Finally they announced, you guys are ready for a "check flight" – which was tantamount to a final exam.

We were the first crew in the training class to get "checked out." We passed easily and were now ready to return to Smokey Hill AFB and start the slow process of upgrading to a combat ready crew.

CHAPTER 11

FINALLY – COMBAT READY

After we completed the B-47 transition training at Wichita and returned to Smokey Hill – we were assigned a B-47 and scheduled to fly every other day - usually Monday, Wednesday and Friday. The non-flying days were used to plan the mission (next flight). A typical flight would be for appx. 8 hours – almost 5,000 miles. We would normally do 2 or 3 navigation legs and 3 or 4 bomb runs. Sometimes we would get an air defense intercept – sometimes we would cut the mission shorter and do a few touch and go landings, et. A couple of times each month we "got a tanker" (did mid-air refueling) and stayed up for over 12 hours.

Since we were a non-combat ready crew, instructors flew with us on every mission. Here again, we were being secretly graded.

It was during one of these training flights that the base called us on the radio and told us to rush back – they said "Lt. Thomas' wife is trying to have a baby." I was scared to death as we returned to base – Frank, a father five times tried to calm me down.

As soon as we landed, I jumped in my car and rushed to the base hospital. I located the doctor my wife had been seeing (Dr. Alvarado) and he said "false alarm – she sitting out in the lobby." I went out and got her – tears were in her eyes – I think she thought she wasn't going to ever have the baby. I took her home and I showered and put on civilian clothes. I cooked supper while she lay on the couch, watched TV, and rested.

We ate supper, watched TV a while, then went to bed. About midnight she started poking me and when I awoke she said she was having labor pains. I quickly got dressed, got her in the car, and raced to the base hospital. Her doctor wasn't on duty (naturally) and that upset her. The young doctor on duty got her file and assured her that he had already delivered a few babies – not to worry. They put her on a cart and rolled her into the delivery room. Meantime, I was a chain smoking nervous wreck.

About 2 a.m. she walked out of the delivery room – smiled, and said "Let's go home." Another false alarm. So we got in the car and went home. I made coffee and stayed up the rest of the night – Caro went to bed and slept. The next morning I called the base and got permission to stay home. (Frank & Jim flew anyway – mostly touch & go (practice) landings.

I dozed off on the couch around midmorning and was really making Z's around noon when Caro wakened me again. She said she was having labor pains again. But I should "time" them before we drove back to the hospital. She said the doctor said when they were at 4 minute internals – it was time. I confess that I yielded to the pressure. Each time the pains came she grimaged and cried out – tears ran down her cheeks. So, when the pains hit 5 minute internals I loaded her in the car and hauled her to the hospital. Dr. Alvarado came out and got her as I checked in – it was almost 1p.m. I didn't finish my first cigarette when Dr. Alvarado came out – smiled, and said "Congratulations dad – you have a son." That feeling is indescribable. So was the feeling a little while later when I went into the room to see Caro and our tiny baby – Michael. He was red as a beet and had a full head of brown hair – and was cute as a button. (and all this happened on August 8th). They stayed in the hospital almost a week and my parents came to help with the new arrival. I went back to flying.

My parents stayed about a week – then Caro's sister came up and stayed about a week – then we were alone with a new baby. Boy, did he change the routine around the Thomas household. Nights before I was scheduled to fly the next day – Caro would get up to feed him – the other nights that was my task. I soon became proficient at changing diapers and operating the washing machine (This was pre disposable diaper days). We didn't own a dryer – had a clothes line in the backyard. When winter arrived - you would hang diapers on the clothes line and in seconds they froze and were stiff as boards. Later, when they were taken off the line they were hung all over the house to dry.

Meanwhile, we were progressing rapidly in our training and by Thanksgiving – were ready for our "check ride" the instructors on this ride were nasty – they did all sorts of tricks to try to mess us up. They cut power on all the right side engines – pull electrical fuses to "knock out" radios and radar, auto pilot, etc. nothing they did rattled us – we fixed it and kept on flying. When we landed from that mission – we were pronounced "combat ready" and elevated to crew R-92. We had a big party to celebrate.

Little did we know what "combat ready" really meant. What it meant was that you had to meet SACs rigid requirements every six weeks – or lose your status, and, as an incentive to do even better, there was always the possibility of earning a "spot" promotion. (A temporary promotion to the next highest rank and related pay hike). We soon learned that SAC was competitive as heck. I don't remember exactly what the six week requirements consisted of but, for sake of illustration, I have prepared the following list.

1. 15 navigation legs of at least 1,000 mile length – maintain average C.E. (circular error) of 2 miles or less.

2. Of the 15 navigation legs, there must be included the following:

   *3 legs using night time celestial navigation

   *3 legs using day time celestial navigation (sun lines)

   *2 legs over water (oceans)

3. 50 bomb runs with average C.E. of 2000 ft or less

4. 1 live bomb drop (every 6 months)

5. 5 air defense intercepts

6. 5 mid air refueling – minimum of 75,000 # of fuel on loaded each time.

7. 30 touch and go landings

8. 1 gunnery range run

9. Pass written test on combat target and weapons

10. 1 max. weight take off – using Jato (rockets)

It soon became apparent that a great deal of a crew's success depended upon the condition of your equipment which in turn depended on the competence and loyalty of the enlisted men who maintained it.

We did everything we could think of to keep our maintenance men happy. Bought them gifts, got them lease passes, gave them parties, etc. etc. When they had to chose between fixing our stuff vs. fixing some Colonel's stuff (one who constantly chewed out their butts) – whose stuff do you think got fixed. Soon, other crews were complaining that we got preferential treatment – particularly when we started passing them in proficiency. Within the first six months. We had been named crew of the month – <u>twice</u>. We started receiving notice throughout SAC. We were one of the crews selected to represent our wing (40TH bomb wing) in SAC wide competition.

CHAPTER 12

STEVE CANYON - NOT

After we left the aircraft at the Martin Marietta plant (Chapter 4) we needed a ride back to Kansas. The U.S.A.F. provided us with a "Desk Jockey" pilot and a small twin engine prop plane (I think it was a C-45) to take us home. The pilot was a young kid from Brooklyn with a high pitched voice. How he even completed flight school and got his wings remains a mystery – he was made for a desk job. He had no flying experience but managed to get in enough flying hours each month to draw his flight pay.

Anyway, we grabbed some flight launches, jumped in a 6 by – and went out to the airplane. Brooklyn was very meticulously going through his pre-flight inspection when we drove up. We introduced ourselves and offered our assistance – which he declined. We waited around till he was finished and climbed aboard. Frank and Jim got in the back seat (planning to sleep) and I got the front seat – next to Brooklyn. He handed me his check list and told me I was co-pilot. As I read the check list – he snappily replied "Roger".

After what seemed an hour – he finally got around to starting the engines. I called the tower and we were cleared for takeoff. It again seemed like it took forever to complete the takeoff roll, get airborne, and climb to altitude. There was no doubt in my mind that jets were the way to go – these old propeller driven planes were slow as turtles.

Anyway, we finally got up to about 10,000 ft. and he got it pointed northwest as we headed to Kansas. Ole Brooklyn's hands never left the controls as we zigged and zagged, up and down through the air. I finally asked "Why don't you put it on autopilot?" He said "No, I wouldn't be flying and getting in my flying requirements for flight pay if I did that." We all chuckled.

After a couple of hours he started getting real nervous. I had been watching the gauges and noted that the needle on the fuel gauge was nearing the Big E so I was a little bit nervous myself. His other problem was that he was lost – which he finally admitted. I had been sort of keeping track of us and knew we were nearing St. Lois so I scanned the horizon and saw it at about 2:00 o'clock. I suggested we land at the St. Louis NAS (naval air station) for fuel. He argued some – said it wasn't air force and wasn't in his flight plan. He had planned to stop at Memphis but flew right past – and we certainly didn't have enough fuel to go back. Frank, the ranking member on board, finally took over and ordered him to land at St. Louis – which he did. He also had his own check list for landing which he would read out loud and repeat the procedure – then say "Roger". His running commentary was both amusing and somewhat frightening – i.e. – throttle back – maintain airspeed of 180 "Roger" called tower "Roger" – left turn to 275° - "Roger" – flaps down "Roger" – gear down "Roger" – crab right, nose up –

easy, easy – nose up a little more – more throttle – more throttle – easy, easy – almost over end of runway – settle down – WHOMP! Brakes – reverse props – slow down – slow down – turn off active – taxi to ad building – cut engines. Then he made the sign of the cross and started giving himself a critique.

We crawled out and went to the men's room to bleed our lizards. We found the coffee pot – got some coffee and lit up cigarettes and started talking to the navy boys while the plane was being refueled.

In a few minutes the fuel truck pulled away and Brooklyn was waving his arms at us – motioning for us to get aboard the plane. We went outside and asked if he didn't want to come in and have a cup of some good navy coffee. He said "No – I don't drink when I'm flying – the caffeine makes me hyper." We sure didn't want him any more hyper – he was driving us crazy as it was.

We loaded immediately and waited for him to complete his pre-flight check list. He crawled aboard and we went through another check list before he finally started the engines again. After awhile we were leveled out and cruising at 10,000 ft again – homeward bound. About 75 miles short of Smokey Hill we ran into a line of typical Kansas thunderstorm clouds. He gritted his teeth and gripped the controls and was obviously going to try to fly through the thunder bumpers. We had done that too many times with a B-47 and knew this little plane would have a heck of a time getting through in one piece. Frank again interviewed and ordered him to fly around the weather – he started to argue and

Frank said "Tommy, you take the controls and Brooklyn – you shut up and sit still.

I turned south and went around the towering cumulus clouds – we had to go about 100 miles extra but that was far better than the probable alternative. When we got into the approach pattern at Smoky Hill I turned the controls back over to Brooklyn. He fought the plane all the way around the pattern and really fought it hard on final – we had winds gusting to 20 m.p.h. He finally pranged it in on his landing and we bounced about 20 feet in the air before he got it back on the ground. But it nevertheless was a successful landing – we all walked away from it.

As we were taxing in he was giving himself a critique – including instructions as to what should have done. Finally we parked by a maintenance hangar and he just sat there for a minute before he finally said "Well, what the heck – I'm no Steve Canyon."

CHAPTER 13

SURVIVAL TRAINING – SAC STYLE

As our crew gained proficiency in the basic skills of bomb delivery we were rapidly approaching the time for survival training - SAC style. The very mention of the word - "Survival" - sent chills up and down your spine. And of course, the "old heads" in the squadron didn't help matters. We heard countless "war stories" from them about how tough "survival training" was going to be. There were several tales of crew members who didn't make it through the training - they either quit or in some cases - died.

However, I had a friend from college in S.A.C. headquarters at Offutt AFB, Nebraska and I went pheasant hunting with him in Nebraska on Thanksgiving holiday. During our visit I expressed my concern about our upcoming "survival training." Bud chuckled and said "Heck Bill, you grew up in the sticks and were in survival training from the day you started walking - you won't have any problems - matter of fact - I expect you'll actually have fun."

He explained that S.A.C. had two survival training schools - arctic and tropical. The arctic survival training was conducted in the winter at Stead AFB, Nevada - in the Sierra Nevada mountains. The tropical survival training was conducted in the Panama Canal Zora in the jungle. The training was similar in both - classroom training followed by several days in the mountains and/or jungle

- surviving off the land and trying to avoid capture. Enlisted men in vehicles were always trying to capture you - if they did - you were brought to a mock P.W., camp and "tortured." The smart thing of course was to avoid capture.

Right before Christmas we got our orders to report to Stead AFB, Nevada in January for arctic survival training. Frank, Jim, and I did a lot of talking about how we were going to "survive." I passed on Bud's suggestions and comments. Jim, a Kansas farm boy agreed "it would be fun," but , Frank, a city boy from Cleveland wasn't so sure about the "fun" part. He obviously wasn't looking forward to a couple of weeks in the fresh mountain air.

The Christmas holidays came and went. My parents came out (from Kentucky) to spend Christmas with us - Caro, myself and our new son Mike. we really enjoyed my parents brief visit and the holiday festivities. My mom is a great cook - so was dad, and they took charge of the Christmas dinner. And of course, Michael was the center of attention. At four months of age, he was already getting spoiled.

On January 4th, we loaded up in Franks station wagon and headed for Stead AFB - outside Reno, Nevada. When we arrived at Stead, it was packed with B-47 crew members from throughout SAC - all there for a good dose of arctic survival training.

We were told at the introduction of the classroom portion of the training that the purpose was to teach us how to survive if we were shot down over Russia and had to make our way out of the U.S.S.R. - on foot. One didn't have to be a map reading expert to look at the map and see just what a challenge that would be - even if it were friendly territory and you spoke the language and had a few rubles in your pocket to buy food occasionally. They explained that we would remain together as crews for the field portion of the training.

About the only things I remember from the classroom training were:

*Stay the heck away from people - hole up during daylight and travel at night.
*The human body is an amazing thing - with very little nourishment it can function for a long time.
*The best medicine when nothing else is available is water - drink all of it you could hold.
*When you get hungry enough - you can and will eat most anything. If it is vegetable and animals eat
   it - so can you. If its animal - you can eat it.
*If it became absolute necessary to contact anyone - seek out the <u>oldest</u> people. They would be more
   apt to help you
*Don't get caught - period! (That's why you carried a .38 caliber revolver).

They also showed us several films and concluded by giving us a very comprehensive tour of the <u>concentration camp</u> where we would be placed if we were caught. It was quite impressionable.

Then came the final exam. Before departing the base they took us by the supply depot and issued the following to each of us:

*1/2 of a silk parachute   *some aluminum foil
*1 pair of snowshoes   *a candle
*Small pkg of salt   *a canteen (for each crew)
*Small pkg of chili powder   *1 can of pemmican
*Small pkg of tea   *10 matches in a waterproof container
*Hunting knife

We were all wearing our winter flying suits, winter flight jackets and caps, and lace up jump boots. We had been searched and had <u>no</u> (zero) personal items with us - just the stuff they issued.

They next loaded us in busses and drove us up into the Sierra Nevada mountains - probably 20 + miles from the base. We unloaded from the busses and each crew boarded a weasel (half track vehicle). The weasels were necessary because the ground was covered by at least three feet of snow. The enlisted man driving the weasel hauled us about 30 miles further into the mountains and left us in a small mountain valley. Before he departed he gave us a very crude hand drawn map (about 8 1/2 x 11) that had an <u>X</u> and a <u>D</u> marked on it. He said we would recognize point D because there was a large wall tent there (a cook tent) and a flag flying on a tall flag pole. He said it was in a wide valley that had few trees as best I could tell, it was appx. 20 miles, as the crew flies, between X and D. Probably closer to 30 miles that we would travel, considering the mountains terrain. He told us we were at point <u>X</u> and had one week to make our way to point <u>D</u> where busses would pick us up and take us back to Stead. He added, all the weasel drivers would be trying to catch us as we made our way to point <u>D.</u> He also said they only hunted during the day so the smart ones only traveled at <u>night</u>. His departing shot was - "don't get caught" and he drove away.

The drone of the weasel engine faded away and it became deathly quiet in that snow cold winter wonderland. It was also extremely cold - probably -10° F or maybe colder. We strapped on the snow shoes and decided to look for a place to hide. I was elected the navigator and leader of our crew so I studied the map and picked out a mountain peak for reference in the direction we would be heading. We started in that direction and were climbing up the side of a small mountain when we found a perfect hiding place - or I should say - it found us. It had taken us a while to master walking with the snow shoes but after a mile or two we got the hang of it. We were in single file and I was breaking the trail. Ahead was a pretty Christmas tree - perfectly symmetrical.

I walked up to the tree and the bottom fell out - it was like falling into a well. The snow had drifted and was about 15 feet deep - the Christmas tree was really the top of about a 20 foot spruce tree. I fell down into the tree - the limbs cushioned my fall and I wasn't hurt. Frank and Jim were peering down into the hole - calling my name. I answered them and assured them I was ok.

Instructed them to cut some of the cord off their parachutes and make a rope about 20 foot long. I told them to tie knots in the rope about every 15-18 inches and to tie one end of the rope to the tree trunk - about at snow level - and to lower themselves down into the hole with me. Frank was the first to try but he had left his snow shoes on and was having trouble. Jim hauled him back to the top and removed his snow shoes and he made it ok. Jim stuck his head in the hole and said - "I hear an engine noise." I said - "it's a weasel - get the heck in here -

quick!" So he did - he just jumped into the hole and came crashing down on top of us.

By using our hunting knives and snow shoes we were able to hack off enough tree limbs and scoop away enough snow to make a small cavern that was quite comfortable. We each wrapped up in the parachutes and lay down. We talked for hours (mostly about women and sex) before we finally dozed off and were soon making z's. Frank was the first to awaken. It was dark inside our cavern so he lit a candle and woke us. By then we were all craving coffee and cigarettes - of which we of course had none. We were starting to get a little hungry also.

I scrounged around and found enough dead limbs, bark, etc. to build a small fire. The smoke almost drove us from our little igloo before the fire burned down some. Next I fashioned a couple of pans from the aluminum foil. I filled one pan with snow and sat it on the fire. In the other pan I placed some pemmican which I "shaved" out of my can and added snow, a pinch of salt, and a pinch of chili powder. I then sat this pan on the fire. When the pan of snow melted and the water started to boil - I added some tea leaves.

In a few minutes we were enjoying our first meal. It was <u>absolutely</u> <u>terrible</u>. Pemmican is beef, pork, and fat - without flavor. Chef boy Ardee would have trouble making it palatable. And the only thing to be said for the tea was it was hot - and wet. We had no cups or dishes so we passed the tea around and took turns sipping and used our knives to try to eat the pemmican. (I decided that the first available wood I came across I'd pick it up and whittle some spoons out of it - which I did the next day).

After the meal it was time to travel so one by one we climbed the tree/rope and popped out on the surface. There was a 3/4 moon and jillions of stars - and it had gotten about 20° colder. We put on our snow shoes and each found a bush for a bathroom. Jim asked "what do you use for toilet paper?" Frank responded "Snow." We regrouped and were ready to move out. It was too dark to see the mountain peak I had selected. However, I had made a mental note that our direction of travel should be a heading of appx. 130° - or southwest. I found the big dipper, north star, arc of capella, etc. and selected a bright star (actually a planet) above the southwest horizon and pointed it out to Frank and Jim. We agreed to stay in a single file and take turns breaking trail - me first. We started cross country and when I got tired, stopped for a break, ate some snow, and then Jim took the lead. The process was repeated all night and we covered perhaps 7 or 8 miles. As it began to get daylight Frank was ready to stop and "camp out" again. We had a meeting and I recommended that we continue on in daylight until we heard one of the weasels or saw one. My idea was (a) as the days passed we would get weaker and be able to cover less distance - therefore it was better to get to the destination point as quickly as possible and find a good hideout near there and just "hide out" till the vehicles showed up to take us back to Stead, (b) I didn't believe the enlisted men would finish their breakfast, drive out from Stead, and be on the "proud" until 10 am or maybe later, and finally (c) I felt we could locate a cave or good shelter in the light. Even though or shelter had been good the previous day I was afraid one of us would break something if we fell into many more holes. Jim agreed with my logic immediately but it took a while to convince Frank.

We moved on and in a couple of hours, Jim, who was in the lead, said "hide, hide" and we hid in some trees. Jim told us there was a road ahead of us and three weasels were parked and the three drivers had a fire built and were huddled around it. We were feeling somewhat cocky and discussed the possibility of slipping up on them, jumping them and tying them up - and stealing the weasels. it was Frank's turn to do the convincing - and he did. It really was a stupid idea.

In about an hour we heard the weasels crank up and drive off. We waited a while longer and slipped up to the road. It had a lot of "weasel" tracks in it and we decided it was an old "logging road" that the weasel drivers had found and used frequently. We further decided to follow the road a ways by staying parallel to it and see what we could find.

After we had traveled about a mile we came upon an old sawmill site. There were several piles of slabs and a big clearing - also a hump which proved to be a garbage pile when we scraped the snow off it. It was heavily wooded around the site and there were no weasel tracks around - I judged it was at least 200 yards to the old logging road. We decided to camp out there. While Jim and I carried slabs (the first cut on a tree - bark on one side - smooth wood on the other) back into the woods and constructed a "lean to" shelter out of them, Frank poked around in the garbage pile.

We cut tree limbs and piled them on the snow for a bed and used them to camouflage our shelter. When Frank joined us he was grinning ear to ear - in his hands were three tin cans. I built a small fire out of old dead wood (practically no smoke) and we filled our newly found treasurers with snow and sat them on the fire - in not time we had boiling water - added tea leaves and were soon sipping hot tea. no one felt like any "chili" so we didn't eat. We talked about girls and sex a while, then wrapped ourselves in our parachutes and went to sleep. We were awakened a couple of times by the sound of weasels as they moved back and forth on the logging road - but they never really came close to us.

Before dark we were all awake and lay there talking about food. From that point forward - the only thing we talked about was <u>food</u> - it can, and did, replace sex on our list of priorities. We were so hungry that we decided to try some more pemmican chili so while Jim built a fire, I sat about shaving some more Pemmican in a can and added snow, salt, and a double dose of the chili powder. We heated snow in the other cans and made more tea.

Either my cooking had improved dramatically or we were so hungry it made no difference. We all wolfed down this batch of chili just as if it were a can of wick fowler special. We sipped the tea, put out the fire, and moved out. I took the lead and had no trouble finding the star (planet) we had followed the night before.

We traveled all night but two things became obvious - one - our pace had slowed dramatically, and two - our breaks had lengthened dramatically also. I don't think we covered more than five miles this night. By dawn we were ready to rest. We found a cluster of trees and just plopped down - scooped a trench in the snow - wrapped up in the parachutes - and promptly went to sleep. We were beat!

Late in the afternoon I was awakened by Jim grilling steaks. I lay there and listened as he described in great detail how, when we got back home, he was going to buy the two largest T-bone steaks in Salina, marinate them, build a big charcoal fire, and grill them to perfection. he would have Joyce, his wife, bake some potatoes and make a large salad to go with his "perfect" meal. After he finished, Frank then described the "perfect" meal his wife Katharine would prepare for him when we got home. It was spaghetti and meat sauce made from an old family recipe and a huge Caesar salad with garlic bread. As I lay there, Saliva built up in my mouth and hunger pains gnawed away at my innards, I couldn't take it any longer so I got unraveled from my parachute and went out to the bushes to be excused. I was amazed to find fresh weasel tracks not more than

100 yards from where we had been sleeping. Thank the lord for trees - otherwise we would have been seen and "captured."

I told Frank and Jim about the fresh tracks and they were likewise surprised - neither of them had heard the weasel pass by. We continued to talk about food for awhile and debated whether or not to eat our last can of pemmican. We had four days remaining before they would pick us up and one can of pemmican. As best I could calculate, we were about half way to our destination. We finally decided it would be better to have three small meals rather than on large one so Jim built a fire and I carefully cut of about 1/3 of the pemmican and prepared to cook another can of chili - except the chili powder was in very short supply and I was forced to ration the seasoning. We made some tea and after our very light supper, we strapped on the snow shoes and moved out toward the southeast.

The terrain was not quite as bad and we apparently had gotten our "second wind" for we covered , I thought, about eight more miles this night. Another factor was the moon was nearing full moon and it was lighter. It was light enough that I could distinguish some deer tracks in the snow - also some other tracks that I wasn't sure of but guessed to be porcupine.

About daylight we came upon an old abandoned log cabin on the side of a mountain. We poked around it awhile and finally decided to spend the day there. The roof was partially caved in and it had been thoroughly pilfered - there was nothing in it of use to us - but at least it offered some shelter from the cold biting wind that began to pickup.

After we settled in I decided to go hunting to see if I could kill something for us to eat. I hacked down a small tree, trimmed it, and whittled a sharp point on one end. neither Frank nor Jim wanted to join me in the hunt so I left. I told them if I didn't return by dark - to go on without me.

A couple of hundred yards from camp I came across some more of the mysterious tracks I had seen the night before and followed them. I became so intent on the hunt that I almost let myself get captured. The animal I was tracking was moving downhill toward a valley. Most of the time it stayed in the woods but occasionally it would cross a clearing.

I was tracking it across a clearing when something (instinct perhaps) cause me to stop and scan the surrounding territory. My heart almost stopped when I saw two weasels parked further down the valley. The two drivers were standing beside one of the vehicles and one of them was pointing toward me.

I remained frozen until I saw them get back into the weasels. My vision was somewhat blurred and I realized that snow blindness was upon me. Too late to worry about snow blindness now - I had to concentrate on escaping. I scanned the mountain I had come down and spotted a rugged, wooded area, that I didn't think the weasels could penetrate and headed for it - as fast as my snow shoes could carry me. We had been told that the drivers did not have snow shoes so basically - if you could get away from the half track weasels - you were safe. The snow was too deep to travel without snow shoes.

The drone of the weasel engines was growing louder and louder as I approached the wooded area - fortunately, I got there first and was able to climb a steep area in the woods. I stopped to rest and listen. The engines were no longer running and it was very quiet - except for my labored breathing and pounding heart. The silence was broken with "here are his tracks" - followed momentarily by "Crap, the snow is too deep to walk and we can't drive in that stuff" - soon followed by "at least we scared heck out of him - let's go" followed by engines starting and the noise gradually fading.

I rested for perhaps thirty minutes and decided to head back to the cabin - the heck with hunting. Further, I had lost my spear that had taken at least an hour to make. It was close to noon and I was tired and sleepy. As I was trudging wearily back toward the cabin I glimpsed movement in a tree up ahead. when I came to the tree I found the source of the movement - a porcupine. He was on a limb just above my reach - happily gnawing away at the tree bark. I looked around for a weapon and was able to break off a fairly solid dead limb from a blown over tree. I fashioned a club from the limb, removed my snow shoes, and climbed far enough up the tree so I could poke the porcupine and dislodge him. He fell to the snow as I scrambled down the tree - I buckled on my snow shoes and pounced on him like a cat. One solid blow to the head and it was all over. I removed a short piece of rope from my pocket, tied it to his forefeet, and drug him back to the cabin - very carefully avoiding his quills.

When I finally reached the cabin, I found Frank and Jim sound asleep. I debated about a half second as to whether or not I should wake them then yelled "Wake up and piss - the world is on fire." They both sat up and Frank said "Damnation Tommy - you scared heck out of me." I said, "You don't know what scared is - let me tell you what I've been through." I then proceeded to tell them of my near capture and concluded with the porcupine episode,

They both got us and examined the porcupine. Jim asked "How do you clean a porcupine?" I responded "Very carefully." We drug him away from the cabin and found a fallen tree. We laid him on his back on the tree and while Frank and Jim held his feet I took my knife and started the surgery to remove his hide and entrails. When I finished we had a naked porcupine.

Since it was going to take a large fire to cook him we decided to wait until dark to start the BBQ. We went back to the cabin and went to sleep. I slept past dark and so soundly that I didn't wake when Jim built a roaring fire in the old fireplace. It burned down to coals and Jim had found a piece of wire and had the porcupine hanging over the coals - roasting away (actually sizzling and popping as the heat melted the fatty tissues).

They woke me after the porcupine was cooked and tea was made. Jim handed me a piece of the porcupine he had sliced of the carcass and he and Frank watched as I bit into it. I chewed on it a little then spat it out Frank asked "What do you think?" I said "Taste like crap" - Frank said "Unanimous." It really taste like <u>pine</u> tree.

I did some experimenting and discovered that if you took a small piece and place in close enough to the coals to actual burn it - the burnt charcoal taste neutralized the pine tree taste and you could actually eat it. We sat around awhile, cooking little tidbits and chewing on them - at least it was something to chew on. Finally, we decided it was time to move so we strapped on snow shoes and headed out. I took the uneaten porcupine, wrapped in foil, with me.

We hadn't traveled more than 3 or 4 miles until Frank started complaining of stomach cramps. We found a blown down tree in some thick woods and improvised a shelter under it. I built a small fire and made some tea. Frank drank most of it and started feeling better - then he went to the bathroom and came back feeling fine. (I think it had been the porcupine working on his delicate city stomach.) He was ready to travel but I told him we were within five miles of point D and had three days and two night remaining before they would pick us up - so we decided to stay there. Besides, it had started to snow and I was a little concerned that we would get lost - visibility was zero with the overcast sky.

Daylight broke and it continued to snow. It seemed we could hear the weasels moving in every direction. We just sat tight all that day - and continued to plan all these fabulous menus for when we got home.

It was approaching dusk and had quit snowing so I built a small fire and started a pot of porcupine chili. I cut very small pieces of porcupine and added it to the pemmican. I also made tea so we ate and sipped tea until dark. We decided that we would try to locate point D this night and then find a good hide out to stay in until pickup time. We strapped on the snow shoes and moved out. Oh yes, I almost forgot, we took south from the fire and made black patches under our eyes to try to prevent snow blindness. It seemed that it had warned up some or maybe we were just acclimated to the cold.

Just before daylight, Frank was breaking trail and called back - "point D ahead." We were moving around the side of a mountain and could see down into a wide valley ahead. There was a tent and the flagpole - a fire was going in the tent and smoke was coming out its chimney. Frank said "Let's go on down and get some coffee, food, and cigarettes from those guys." Jim and I said "No - we've come too far to get caught now." While we were standing there arguing, we could see three men trudging across the snow toward the tent they were coming from another direction. (apparently they had dropped the flight crews off in all directions - so we wouldn't "join up"). Frank said "see there - those guys are going to the tent." About that time, someone emerged from the tent and got into a weasel and drove out to meet the crew - and they got into the weasel and it drove off. Frank said "They just got captured." Frank didn't argue further.

We decided to get a little higher on the mountain and try to find a good hideout with a view of the tent. After a few minutes of travel we stopped and Jim said "I smell wood smoke". We all sniffed the air and concluded it came from ahead and above us. We moved on in that direction and soon saw the entrance to a cave with a small fire burning inside it. We cautiously approached and a voice inside said "Who's out there?" We said "Three starved and ragged airmen." They laughed and said "Come on in brothers of the thin air - make yourselves at home."

We took off our snow shoes and entered the cave and introduced ourselves. They were a B-47 crew from Davis Monthan AFB, Arizona - Col. Wade, Capt. Refues, and Capt. Lee They had decided to do the same thing we had decided - get there a day early and hideout.

The rules were that you couldn't report to the tent at point D until noon the next day or later. That meant we had all this day, tonight, and a half day tomorrow until we could check in. Col. Wade suggested that we wait until either (a) all the weasels had left the area or (b) darkness the next day to check in. He had been told by an officer who had been through the program that most crews were caught the last day - trying to get to the tent. All the weasels returned to the tent the last day and had "Easy pickings" from the over anxious crews who got caught out in the open.

We pooled our food supplies and I was elected to prepare our last meal. I had the following to work with:

* 1 1/2 cans of pemmican
* 1/2 of a porcupine
* 2 full pkg of chili powder
* 2 1/2 pkg of salt
* Bag of pinion nuts
* 2 pkg of tea

We still had our three tin cans so I carefully cut the porcupine in very small pieces and "shaved" the pemmican in a can. I also cut up a couple of handfuls of the pinion nuts and dumped them along with the slat and chili powder into the pot - actually it took two cans. We made tea in the other. After the cooking we fashioned plates from the remaining foil and sat down to a feast - it really didn't taste that bad. then we passed the community tea pot around and everyone got a sip or two.

While we were eating we watched four more weasels drive up to the tent - there were now ten vehicles parked down there. Captain Lee said - "Look over yonder - there's another crew about to get caught." We watched as the same drama unfolded - three men walking single file toward the tent - a driver emerge from the tent, get in a weasel - go pick them up - and haul them off. This happened two more times before dark. We felt safe and smile in our little cave.

Before retiring for the night we had a contest to see who could describe the greatest meal. It seems the other crew had been talking about food also. Frank won with his Italian meal.

The next morning we got up and were eager to head to the tent - but Col. Wade insisted we sit tight - and he was right. We watched crew after crew get captured out in the open area. About mid morning we heard a siren and watched as an ambulance raced past the tent and up the valley. A while later it raced back through the area. (We learned later that a Major from Hunter AFB, GA had suffered a heart attack - and died on the way to the hospital).

The Colonels wisdom and our patience was finally rewarded around three in the afternoon - all the weasels were gone from the area so we strapped on our snow shoes and walked to the tent. We were the first crews to arrive safely. Some General was there and he shook our hands and whooped us on the back. We were much more anxious to get to the hot coffee, bacon, and scrambled eggs - and cigarettes!

We quickly made a startling discovery however - we could eat no more than a bite or two! Our stomachs had shrunk down to the size of a walnut perhaps and couldn't hold any food. We could sure drink the coffee and smoke those cigarettes through - and nibble from time to time on the food.

Shortly after our arrival - other crews began to check in at the tent. Before long, it was packed. By about 4 pm the weasels returned and started shuttling us to the busses which were waiting at the highway. We were among the first to return to Stead.

The first thing we did was take photos of one another - what a motley looking crew. Long beards , dirty teeth, and just dirty - period. the showers were in a separate building and there was about a foot of snow on the ground. It must have been a sight to see us undress, grab a towel, razor, and clean shorts, and wack bear assed naked through the snow to the showers. We emerged clean shaven and clean. We put on our uniforms and headed to the mess hall.

The cooks had everything imaginable prepared - steak, chicken, pork chops, stew, soups, vegetables, etc, etc. But we still couldn't hold any food. I asked a cook if they had a scale - he directed me to one in the kitchen. I weighed and discovered I had lost 34 pounds. Sooo - if you want a sure fire diet .... try pemmican and porcupine.

We hung around the mess hall for a couple of hours and nibbled - but mostly drank coffee and smoked cigarettes.

We finally decided to go to Harrolds Club in Reno - gamble a little - then return to the base for some sleep before heading back for Kansas - survivors!

CHAPTER 14

THAT NIGHT IN RENO

Jim and I were rank amateurs when it came to gambling. I had played a little poker in college but Jim hadn't even done that. Frank, on the other hand, was an "old pro."

When we got to Harold's club I checked my wallet and had $42. Jim had about the same. Frank had about $200. We followed Frank and he went straight to the crap table. We watched him lose his $200 – quickly. Jim discovered the one armed bandits and I found a bingo game.

Frank cashed a check and jumped back into the crap game. Jim soon lost his money and joined Frank. Meanwhile, I sipped on a beer and played bingo - $5 per game. A strange thing happened – I started <u>winning</u> at bingo - $50 per game. It seemed I was winning at least every other game we played.

Jim came back to the bingo game to join me and his eyes popped out when he saw my winnings. I won again while he was there. The he left – and I won again.

The next thing I knew, both Frank and Jim joined me and Frank "hit me up for a loan." He was down a few hundred at the crap table and they wouldn't cash any more of his checks. I gave him all my winnings – about $400 – and he went back to the crap table.

I stayed with bingo and won twice more. He returned and "borrowed" another $100. This went on for about two more hours. I won a few more games but Frank always returned to "borrow" my winnings.

I was getting very sleepy so I decided to quit so we could go back to the base. I had won another game but stuck the 50 bucks in my wallet. I joined Frank and Jim at the crap table in time to watch Frank lose the last of the borrowed money. He wanted to borrow more but I convinced him I too was broke – so we went back to the base.

We stopped at the mess hall and had some soup and ice cream – then went to bed.

The next morning we headed back to Kansas. I was the only one with any money so I bought the gas and food on the way home. Frank was a little peeved that I hadn't loaned him my last dollar – but glad in a way that I hadn't. We had gone without food long enough on this trip.

The survival training was good in several ways – first, it toughened us physically and mentally. We now knew we could survive most anything. And it brought us much closer as a crew – we knew we could depend on one another.

But – it was still good to get home to a warm bed and cuddling wife – and home cooked meals.

CHAPTER 15

TARGET ASSIGNED

When we got back from survival training we were about as good at our jobs as anyone in the squadron. We were good enough that they assigned a target (and secondary target) in Russia that we were to destroy should war break out.

We all had "top secret" clearances and all the target information was kept under heavy guard in the "war room" – a concrete block, particularly buried, building that stood alone in an isolated area on the base. The building had movie projectors, slide projectors, etc.

We always went together as a crew to study our target information at the war room. Even though they had fairly thick file on both targets - our primary target and secondary target – I'm sure the information was archic compared to the information later developed by our spy satellites. We had photos, aerial photos, radar photos, engineering drawings, and various other bits of information about our targets. After hours of concentrated study – we knew more about our targets than we did about our own base.

Here again, we were sworn to secrecy (I suppose for life) about this information. I think I can safely say that our primary target was a nuclear plant in the Ural mountains and our secondary target was an airbase.

The intelligence boys pumped us full of propaganda. We were told that after we hit the target there were auxiliary airfields all around Russia where we could land and refuel – and get ammo, food, and water for our return trip to the U.S.A. We were also told that there would be plenty of tankers to refuel us over the Atlantic on the way back.

Our studies included the planned route we would take to the target along with alternative escape routes.

Early in the game when the only anticipated resistance we would encounter on the way to the target was standard anti aircraft fire and mig fighter planes – they told us our chance of delivering the bomb and returning home safely was 90 + percent.

As time passed and they updated the information, they knew we weren't dumb so they kept dropping the aforementioned % - 80%, 70%, 60%, 50% - then lower – when it got below 50% we had to change our strategy (see Chapter 24).

There were two reasons our expected success (survival) percentage kept dropping. First, the Russians were staying abreast of us in both aircraft and missile technology. Their newer MIGS with afterburners were capable of getting to our attitude and catching us. (and there were two air bases that we would fly near on our way to our target). And the current maps we were studying showed ground to air missile sites encircling both targets. They showed us film of missile tests and there was no doubt those babies could knock a B-47 out of the sky.

Of course we weren't sitting still either – new radar jamming and electronic counter measure equipment were always being installed on the B-47's. We had added extra fuel tanks (drop tanks) and there was an improved jato system (rocket assisted take off). But in future alerts if we got airborne and headed toward our targets – you really puckered up if you stopped to think about what you were really doing.

There was one time that I felt we were really going all the way. It happened while we were stationed in England. I think the communist had just overthrown the government in Syria – or some such crisis. Anyway, we went on alert and scrambled. We flew to our position cn the go/no go line and were circling – ready to head for the target. It seemed we were there for an eternity before we got the coded signal which meant – false alarm – come on home. (We could not proceed past the go/no go line until we received a confirming signal – in code-to do so. As juiced up as we were – it still amazes me that some crew didn't screw up and fly on in to their target and unload. It would have <u>been possible</u> in the early years. Probably not in later years - if the migs didn't get them, the missiles would have. (I assume the USA would have warned Russia that one screwed – up and was on the way – maybe not – who knows – or cares now).

CHAPTER 16

ALERT!

We had not been on combat ready status more than a couple of weeks when my phone rang at 3:00 am. I answered and the voice at the other end said "This is Captain Smith – we are on red alert – report to your aircraft immediately." I replied "Yes sir" and hang up. The call woke Caro who asked "What is going on?" I told her we were on red alert and I had to get to the base <u>immediately</u> – war could be starting. She started to cry as I grabbed underwear, socks, and car keys. I threw on a robe, jumped into the car. And peeled rubber as I left the driveway. Indian Village was about two miles from the base and that two mile stretch became a race track as flight crews raced to the base.

I parked at the squadron, locked the car, and raced to my locker and put on my flying gear and grabbed my briefcase. I didn't lace my boots and nearly fell several times as I ran clumsily to our plane. Frank was already there doing preflight. I grabbed his check list and helped him until Jim arrived about 3 minutes later. I climbed aboard and got settled in – Frank and Jim were right behind. In seconds the engines were fired up and we taxied into position for takeoff we were third from last in our squadron to takeoff.

We started climbing out toward the northeast and leveled off at 39,000 ft. (as the plane burned off fuel it became lighter and naturally increased altitude – the highest we ever took a B-47 was 50,000 ft). We could see aircraft ahead and knew they were other B-47's – headed for Russia.

After a few hours we hooked up with a tanker near Goose Bay, Labrador and took on enough fuel to get us to our target. The tanker we latched onto was an old KC-97 (propeller powered). The only way to refuel with a KC-97 was to hookup and head down in a dive – that was the only way to keep the 97 above our stall speed. It was right sporty getting fuel from a KC-97 – later when the jet tankers (KC-135) became operational – no sweat. After refueling, we continued eastward. There was radio silence. We were nearing great Britain when we finally got a radio message "false alarm" – return to base." We did a 180° turn and headed west – back to Kansas.

Since we were one of the last to takeoff we were one of the first to land. When we taxied in and parked, Captain Smith (security) met us as we climbed out of the plane and told us to report to squadron headquarters for debriefing.

When we got to squadron headquarters, Colonel Hempleman was furious. Our squadron did poorly in getting its plans in the air. He took the opportunity to vent his anger on us. He chewed on us for at least 10 minutes – until another crew showed up for him to chew on. We went through debriefing and found that we (a) were late in getting airborne (which we already knew) (b) did not have all the proper – equipment (Jim and I had forgot our .38 revolvers) (c) were not properly attired (my boots were unlaced); and (d) hooked up with the wrong tanker. In short, we had failed on our first alert.

The next day we sat down and planned on how to improve our response - in case there was another alert. (and of course, there were many, many, more). The rumor was that a flock of geese had been picked up on the <u>dew</u> line radar – who thought it was Russian planes – thus the alert. Who knows – our job was not to question why; it was to deliver bombs when directed to do so – no questions asked.

CHAPTER 17

EVERYTHING WAS NORMAL – THE SMOKE WAS BLACK AND THE FLAME WAS RED

We continued to fly and become more and more proficient due in large part to the high quality of our maintenance – particularly on the bombing system. Our C.E.A. – average circular error of the misses was about 900 ft. – not bad when you consider the fact that the hydrogen bomb we carried would completely destroy a city the size of Houston. All you really had to do was drop it close. A few months after we had become a combat ready crew - we were advanced to lead crew status (L-92).

Even though flying was serious business – it had its exciting and its lighter moments. Here are a few of the incidents I remember.

These happened during SAC wide competitive events in which we were one of the crews representing the 40th bomb wing.

The way the competition was set up was that SAC would lay out the course and set up the test measuring devices (usually ground radar) and the planes flew the course – one by one - about 5 minute intervals. This was called a "bomber stream." To illustrate the course might begin at Chicago (Point A) and you flew to rejovic, Greenland (Point B) – (This nav leg would be graded) – you had a mid air refueling in that vicinity (again – graded – amount of fuel/time) – then you flew to Miami, Florida (Point C) (another graded Nav leg) – next to Orlando, FL (IP) and made a bomb run on St. Petersburg, FL (Point D) (graded), next to co-ordinates in the Gulf of Mexico (Point E) where you dropped a dummy bomb and fired the local machine guns on a floating target with a radar reflector on it – then a bomb run on Dallas (Point F) – (graded) – and a final nav leg to Kansas city (Point G) with an air defense intercept at the end of this leg. You returned to home base for debriefing and a critique.

Although our crew never won a SAC wide competition – we always finished in the top 25% of SAC – not bad when you consider we were always up against much more experience crews.

It was on a competition on a course similar to the one described above that we messed things up for everyone behind us. The bomb we dropped on the floating target was an old a-bomb case filled with concrete - probably weighed 6,000 pounds. We hit the target and sunk it – we heard the next couple of planes behind us fussing because they couldn't locate the target.

In another competition our aircraft developed an electrical fire I put it out with a fire extinguisher. It was scary but no big deal really. However, when we landed and were debriefing one of the officers asked Frank "How did it go Captain?" Frank snapped back "Heck, everything was normal. The smoke was black and the flame was red."

Weather was another sporting proposition. Even though the B-47 was a large heavy aircraft and very powerful – it was often overmatched in a challenge with mother nature.

In the hot summer, towering cumulus clouds would build up quickly in Kansas. Often, tornados danced out of them. We had been up on a long mission one day (about 12 hours) and were tired and hungry as we returned to the base. However, the base was covered by those darn towering cumulus clouds. The tower suggested we land at an alternate field - they recommended Little Rock AFB, Arkansas. Frank said, were running out of fuel and have to land or get a tanker. The tower came back and said "no tankers in the area – land at your own risk." Frank said on the intercom – "Hold on boys – this is going to be a rough ride" – then he nosed the B-47 over and we dove into a gigantic cloud.

Rough does not adequately describe that ride. First we hit rain – then hail – it sounded like 726 boys were shooting rocks at us with sling shots. Then an updraft which threw us about 1000 feet straight up – next a down draft that took us 2000 feet straight – down. The wings (which had a 14 ft built in travel at the tips) were flapping up and down like a buzzard's wings. We finally made it to the landing pattern – the tower had us on radar and kept asking Frank to slow down – he said "heck fire, if you were up here in this crap – you'd be in a hurry to get on the ground." He took her full blast almost to touchdown. When we finally parked and got out – it looked like Paul Bunyon had taken a ball peen hammer and beat the heck out of our airplane. But we made it.

The next time we encountered this cloud situation – we were coming in from the west. We had plenty of fuel so Frank decided we would fly around the clouds. I set up the radar so I could monitor the clouds and was to tell Frank if I spotted an opening we could slip through. None showed up and now and again Frank would ease over closer to the clouds – then St. Elmos fire would start running up and down the wings and he would back off. Finally we came to the end of the line of towering Q's – we were just north of El Paso, Texas – and very low on fuel. Jim suggested we land at Davis Monthan AFB. Arizona – so we headed west. It was dark by now - and probably just as well. Davis Monthan – was surrounded by mountains – it was like landing in a soup bowl. They had good radar and radar operators who talked us down safely. I had looked at the charts and saw what we were getting into so I monitored that landing very carefully on my radar.

We spent that night in the BOQ and the next morning when we lined up for takeoff Frank said "Look at those mountains – they encircle this field – how the heck did we ever land here." In leaving, you had to sort of spiral your way to altitude to get over the mountains. We all made a mental note to avoid Davis Monthan in the future.

The Kansas winters presented a problem which was solved in a rather unique way. The problem was ice – the solution was the heat generated by the six jet engines of the B-47. When it rained, snowed, or sleeted – the B-47 would become covered with ice because they were parked out in the open . The maintenance boys would park two B-47's tail to tail – leaving enough distance for another B-47 to pass between them. They could then fire up the 12 jet engines on the parked B-47's and tow the others between them, one by one, to de ice them so they could fly. After they had been thus de-iced. They were warm and comfy when you climbed around.

But the airplane was not always comfortable. Most people don't realize how cold it gets at high altitude. At 40,000 ft – where we lived – the air temperature was about - 20° F. The planes were equipped with the first heat pumps invented. These pumps provided heat in the winter and cold air in the summer. But they sometimes "malfunctioned." The cockpit area was not insulated and the "skin" of the aircraft got extremely cold. We normally carried boxed flight lunches and there were literally hundreds of times when my box lunch would slide over to the side and come to rest touching the outside skin. Talk about frozen food – when you bite down into a chicken drumstick – it was like biting a tire tool. You would have to put whatever you ate next to your body for about an hour before you could eat it.

Since we were normally in the air 8 to 12 hours each time we flew we had certain biological needs. For No. 1 - the plane was equipped with "relief" tubes. These were rubber hoses with a small funnel and a value near the funnel - the other end extended to the outside air. For No. 2 - we carried a "honey bucket" - not much more sophisticated than a 5 gallon can. Whoever used the honey bucket first had to clean it when we landed. It was probably the least used piece of equipment on the plane. The relief tubes were never perfected - at high altitude they would freeze up and when you used them - the amber liquid would blow back at you (because of cabin pressure). It wasn't much relief.

Another problem that never got fixed on the B-47 (or any military aircraft) was the "odor" problem. They always smelled horrible - exhaust fumes, fuel (JP4) fumes, stale farts, and stale piss. We sometimes brought a can of room deodorizers along to spray the cabin good - then it smelled like a pine forest for a day or two.

Jet streams were another problem - until you got used to them. Very little was known about jet streams until we came along and started flying at the 40-50,000 altitude levels. The best way I can describe them is they were like a "river" of very fast flowing air - over 100 m.p.h. - which flowed in an eastward direction over the north American continent. They migrated southward as winter approached. You could actually feel it when you entered one form the side - and if you watched the outside temperature gauge - which dropped about 15% when you entered a jet stream. The effect of a jet stream on the aircraft should be obvious. If it hit you in the tail - your air speed went from about 600 mph to 700 mph $\pm$. The opposite effect occurred when you were hitting it head on - your speed dropped to about 500 mph - you felt like you were crawling. And of course, if it hit you on the side - it would blow you the heck off course in just a couple of minutes. It was your worse fear that you would bump into a jet stream at the termination of a nav leg - and they were tough to compensate for on bomb runs - but you learned to handle them.

The B-47 did not have "reverse" thrust on its six jet engines - thus, the runways were 10,000 ft long. To assist in stopping that big bird we had a "drag chute" that we would pop when we hit the runway. The brakes were also very good.

My most frightened moments on a B-47 involved getting one stopped one afternoon at Smokey Hill. We had been on a normal mission (about 8 hours) and were landing at Smokey Hill. There was light snow on the ground when we took off but it had been snowing all that day and was snowing when we landed. The tower tried to get us to land at an alternate field but as usual - we were too low on fuel for that alternative. The snow plows had been busy all day, trying to keep the runways clear. But the tower warned us that there was a lot of snow and ice on the runway. No sweat - with the drag chute and brakes we could surely stop within 10,000 ft. - right? Wrong!!!

The instant we hit the runway Frank said "Drag chute." Jim popped the drag chute but nothing happened. Frank said - "Jim, hit the drag chute" Jim said "I did". Frank said "It didn't deploy." Jim said "Look back there - we're dragging a block of ice." (The drag chute had gotten we and frozen into a block of ice). Frank said "Aw crap - get on the brakes with me." All I could hear was their heavy breathing - looked out the window and saw the markers zipping past in a blur - I knew we were moving down the runway too fast. Frank called the tower and explained our problem. They dispatched the emergency vehicles and a command came from the senior tower officer "ground loop the aircraft." Frank said "buckle up and hold on" and the aircraft turned sideways as we skipped and skidded to a stop. The plane was leaning at an angle and resting on the left wing - the left outrigger gear had snapped off. Frank yelled - "We can't get out the door - Jim, blow the canopy." Blam - the canopy was blasted off and we scrambled out of there like scared rabbits - the fuel odor was strong and we knew we had either ruptured a fuel tank or broken a fuel line. By then, the fire engines and ambulance had us surrounded and were squirting foam on the plane, we ran about a hundred yards in the snow and stopped and looked back. Nothing happened - no explosion or fire - Thank God! Just three very scared bird men!

CHAPTER 18

ROTATION

About the time we became a combat ready crew, SAC came up with a new tactic. The common description for the tactic was "rotation." In practice, the tactic involved moving a <u>complete</u> bomb wing from its U.S. home base to a base overseas - most of which were in England. (i.e. Lakenheath, Brize Norten, Mendenhall, Greenham Common, etc.) The wing would replace a wing that was already there and in 90 days it too would be replaced and would return (rotate) to its home base in the USA. In case what I just said escaped you, let's think about it and see what moving an entire bomb wing across half the continent and the Atlantic ocean involved. A bomb wing consisted of 3 bomb squadrons plus all the support group. Each squadron had 15 active B-47 is plus a couple of spares. That's 30 pilots and 15 observers in flying personnel. The maintenance personnel probably numbered around 50 and the administrative staff probably numbered another 50. That's a total of about 145 people and about 50 bombers - plus a lot of equipment. (Fuel trucks, tow vehicles, 6 x 6 trucks, ambulances, jeeps, etc.)

Our turn to ship out overseas came around. I tried to convince Caro to take baby Michael and either go home and stay with her parents or go stay with my parents until I got back. She refused. Instead, she called her younger sister, Minerva, who came to Saliva to stay with them.

One the appointed day, we literally loaded up and headed for England. As we were flying across the ocean toward England - specifically Greenham Common AFB (about 60 miles west of London) another bomber wing (I think from Madill AFB) had departed Greenham Common AFB and were headed back to the USA ("Rotating"). We tried aerial refueling near Nova Scotia. But the tanker never showed up (or if he did - someone else got him). We finally made contact with a tanker about 200 miles east (out over the Atlantic) and headed toward him. We found him and refueled - then proceeded to England. A few hours later we saw the coast of Ireland on the horizon and before you knew it, we were in the landing pattern at Greenham Common. We would be stationed at this base for the next 90 days - until we "rotated."

We landed and parked - an enlisted man in a 6 by (truck) picked us up and took us to the debriefing and processing center. Naturally, it was raining. There, we received our room assignments, exchanged currency, etc. Then we were taken to the BOQ where we unloaded and unpacked. Jim and I were roommates, Frank had his own room right across the hall. We showered and went to bed and promptly fell asleep. It had been a long day and we were very tired.

We awoke the next morning - hungry as wolves. It took us a while to wake Frank and get him up. Finally, Frank got up and got dressed. We asked him

"Where do we go to eat?" He said "The Officers Club." We finally located someone who knew where The Officers Club was located - it was on the other side of the runway - too far to walk. We stood outside the BOQ, trying to decide how we could get to the Officers Club. Finally, a Captain (one of our doctors) came out and got into an ambulance. We stopped him and he gave us a ride to the Officers Club.

The Officers Club had formally been an English estate - it was an imposing two story brick structure located on a hill overlooking the town of Newberry. The grounds were very manicured. We went inside and it was crowded - finally we got a table and ordered bacon, eggs, muffins (English naturally), and coffee. When our food was served - we were in for a terrible disappointment. The bacon was almost raw - the scrambled eggs were made from powdered eggs - and the coffee was weak. The cooks were British, and the food was terrible - and it didn't improve. I'm convinced you could easily starve to death in England. Other meals were no better - the beef they served was from Argentina - pure grass fed and tough. The fish was undercooked, and I don't eat mutton - nor do I care for kidney pie.

But we soon made the adjustments necessary to survive. Many of the older heads in the squadron, including Frank, had been stationed in England during World War II and they were a big help. There was a well stocked BX (base exchange) on the base. There, we purchased a hot plate, a few pots and pans, coffee pot, dishes, etc. Plus a 5 pound can of Maxwell House coffee, some Campbell soup, pork and beans, Vienna sausage, etc. Thereafter, a vendor on a bicycle showed up in front of the B.O.Q. each morning with a wide selection of French pastries.

Our breakfasts in the future were normally home brewed coffee made in our room and French pastries. Lunch was usually a box flight lunch - even if we weren't flying, and supper was either Vienna sausage and beans in our room or a hamburger steak at the Officers Club. That was the only thing they cooked at the Officers Club that was fit to eat. And I went back into the kitchen and taught them how to fix the hamburger steaks. (lots of chopped onions and salt and pepper before they fried them.) (Also, I convinced the cooks to fry the French fries until they were brown i.e. fully cooked).

The next day we visited a "used" car lot just outside the gate at the base. Frank bought an Austin (car), and Jim and I each bought motorcycles - mine was a Royal Enfield. We were now mobile and more comfortable.

Things started to settle down into a routine - we were on alert for three days on flying duty for three days - then off for one day. We normally flew two missions while we were on duty. The weather was almost always bad and nearly every landing was radar controlled.

Generally, our missions were of shorter duration while we were overseas. I suppose that was partly to conserve fuel and partly because there was so much restricted and/or unfriendly air space over there. Further, there weren't many scoring sites set up for bomb runs. Most of the time we made our bomb run on London.

Our first bomb run over London was a complete disaster. We made the bomb run from the south. As we approached London, it completely filled the radar scope (25 mile range). I had never seen anything so huge on the radar scope before. When I had studied the target during mission planning - it did not look anything like what I was seeing on the radar set. However, I knew from my study of a conventional map that the target was northeast of "downtown" London. However, our radar was so fine turned - we were picking up all the suburbs. The fact is - I couldn't locate my target. But finally convinced myself that strong return in the northeast quadrant had to be it. I put the cross hairs (+) on the target and completed the bomb run. When we got the bomb score Frank said "Crap Bill - that was a boon doggler (a miss of more than five miles) Frank elected to "abort" the mission and we returned to Greenham Common.

The next day we had to report to a board of inquiry - headed by the wing commander, Colonel Low. Anytime you had a Boon doggler - this was standard procedure. Frank was the first one "on the carpet". He tried to protect me by blaming the equipment. (I knew they had the equipment calibrated after we landed and it checked out ok - I could also tell from the eyes of Col. Low that he didn't buy Frank's story) then I heard "Lieutenant Thomas - front and center." I jumped up - approached the board of inquiry - and gave them my best salute. Colonel Low said "At ease" - but I couldn't very well get at ease in the spot I was in - deep do do. Colonel Low said "Lieutenant" - do you think your equipment was at fault?" I said "No Sir." He inquired "What was the problem?" I said "It was all my fault." Colonel Low said "We know that - but what was the problem? One never knows how these thoughts develop in your sub-conscious - but they do - and without thinking, I blurted out "It was a bad, bad case of cranial rectitus Sir."

The response broke them up. After they quit laughing, Colonel Low looked me in the eye and said "Lieutenant, that is the most honest answer I've ever heard at an inquiry - you men may go now." We started to leave and Colonel Low called out "Don't do that again" I said "No Sir."

For the next few days we were the laughing stock of the squadron - and not very popular. Our squadron commander, Colonel Hempleman had called us into his office and chewed butts - he said we had the whole squadrons average C.E. so high that he would probably get a call from General Lemay.

Frank, Jim, and I talked it over and decided to take matters in our own hand. We decided to "camp out" over London. The next day and make as many bomb runs as possible - at least as long as the C.E. was acceptable (under 5000 ft.) so we did. The next day we made 10 bomb runs over London with an average C.E. of 1905 ft. Colonel Low wrote us a nice "Thank You" letter. (See next page) -

HEADQUARTERS
United States Air Force
N.Y., N.Y

40C

7 August 1957

Subject: Letter of Appreciation

To: 1STLT Billy R. Thomas, No 2206175
    45th Bombardment Squadron
    40th Bombardment, Wing, Medium
    167, New York, New York

1. I have been informed of the fact that on 31 July 1957 you and your crew flew an R31 mission during which you reached a total of Ten (10) reliable a.c.e. runs with a.c.e. of Nineteen hundred and five (1905) feet.

2. This effort is exemplary and is indicative of the spirit and attitude we desire in all our crews. It is especially commendable in view of the fact that you did not need these runs for reliability but merely strove to improve your reliability factor and aid
your squadrons 50-8 effort. Such results reflect much credit on you and your crew.

3. I wish to extend to you my sincere appreciation for a job well done.

4. It is my desire that a copy of this letter become a part of your field personnel records.

                                                Andrew B. Low
                                                Colonel. UCAF
                                                Commander

We were now back in good graces at the squadron and with our wing commander - at least temporarily. Then we screwed up again.

A couple of missions later we decided to fly north to the arctic area. We also decided to fly close to the Russian border - just to see what was there. (no one ever told us to fly close to Russia - nor did they tell us not to). So I planned the mission to go north from England, skirt the northern most point of Scandinavian (North Point), then head west southwest and fly between a Russian island named Kolguyev and Russia before turning north again toward the north pole. On the way back we planned to come through the gunnery range west of the Shetland Islands. So Jim could fire the twin 50 caliber machine guns and get that requirement off the list.

Everything went fine until we passed Kolque and turned north. Jim came on the intercom and said "Boys, we got company." We looked out to the right and flying just off our wing tip was a Russian mig - we could see the pilots face. He was signaling with his hands - pointing down - like he was yelling us to land. Frank Shock his head no. Jim gave him the old finger (were #1 salute). The Russian pilot seemed confused. Frank said "Turn on the radar gun controls Jim - if that S.O.B. follows us we'll shoot his butt down". He then put the B-45 in a shallow turn to the left, pulled the nose up, and went to full throttle as we climbed away from the mig. The Russian peeled right and headed away from us. We continued on our mission. On the way back when we entered the restricted gunnery range - Jim fired a few rounds through the guns. Then they fired automatically - radar controlled (Jim had forgotten to turn the radar gun control off). Jim said "Heck fire, there's a "target" on the radar." Frank shouted "Turn it off!" About the same time this voice came over the radio "Blimey, the bloody bastard is shooting at me." Then a very British accented voice came on the radio "American aircraft - break contact, break contact." Then "Yes Sir - but I think I'm hit."

The next day, we were back on the carpet - facing Colonel Low and the board of inquiry. We were really concerned this time - we didn't know if we were being investigated for flying top close to Russia or for shooting at the British fighter. We decided to keep quiet, volunteer nothing, and just answer their questions. Jim was the first to testify. it quickly became obvious that the problem was the British fighter. Frank and I looked at each other and breathed sign of relief. Then it was my turn and they questioned me about our exact position when the guns were fired. I testified that we were over 10 miles inside the restricted area (gunnery range) before a shot was fired. (That fact was verified by ground radar). Colonel Low asked "Any cranial rectitis this time?" In unison we said "No Sir." The board finally admitted that the British fighter was at fault - and not us. They said the Air Force would pay to repair the couple of bullet holes in the British plane and that would be the end of it. They let us go again with Colonel Low getting in his last lick "Don't do that again" - response "No Sir".

There was another flying incident that we later got a few good laughs about - although at the time it really wasn't that funny.

At the end of a mission we did a navigation leg - really a triangle. England to Iceland to a point in the Atlantic Ocean then to our base at Greenham common. It was during daylight hours so I was navigating with the sextant using sun lines.

We had almost completed the nav leg and I had done my last fix and given Frank a final A.H. and E.T.A. heading - direction and estimated time on arrival. We were rapidly approaching the E.T.A. and neither Frank nor Jim could get a response from their radio calls.

Frank called me and said "Today, no one will answer the radio - what do you see on radar? I responded "Nothing - just a clean sweep." (That is what it looks like over the ocean - no target reflections - just sweeping clean).

Frank said "We got a problem - I'm going to do a 360 - you check your last calculations." In the meantime, I had looked out the window and saw that there was complete cloud cover below us. I rechecked and told Frank I was sure of my calculations. There was a long period of silence.

Frank called back and said "Tommy, I'm going to fly South on 180 and see if we can find Africa."

Jim came on and said I think I've figured out the problem - we've lost A.C. (alternating current). Frank said - "Hit the IFFR switch." Jim did and in no time a British fighter popped through the clouds and came up beside us and signaled to follow him. We dove down through the clouds and came out of them - right over the airfield.

One night we were heading back to the base and were crossing the English channel - it was one of those nights that was pitch black. Suddenly, we heard a whump! and the plane shuddered. I got on the intercom and asked "What the heck was that?" Frank said "It's nothing - somebody just crossed in front of us and we hit the jet wash." (In fact, we very nearly had a mid air collision - we have no idea what or who the other aircraft was - it was at the wrong altitude in any case).

On another flight we were flying over Spain and developed some engine problems - some serious engine problems. Frank said "Jim, Bill - find us a place to land this big bird - Quick!" I grabbed a chart and computed our position quickly and got on the horn "Frank, there is a Spanish airbase at Zaragoza - about 100 miles at 90 degrees." Jim chimed in almost immediately with "I've got Zaragoza on the radio - they said we can land there." Frank rolled her to the right and we headed for Zaragoza. We made a straight in approach and were landed and parked within 15 minutes. This base was one of Franco's air defense bases - equipped with U.S. built F-86's. There was a complement of U.S. Air Force maintenance personnel stationed there. They immediately had the cowlings off our two inboard right engines and soon found the problem - broken fuel line. One of them said - "This is going to take an hour or so to fix - if you guys are hungry - there's a good restaurant in town." We told him we were starved for good food. One of the men got a jeep and took us into town. The restaurant was on the town square. There was a wood fire burning in a fireplace directly in the center of the restaurant - a chef was tending the fire. We were seated and handed menus - in Spanish. The waiter came to take our order - he spoke Spanish. I said - grande biftek, legumbres, ensalada, pan and vino - trece. He smiled and wrote it down - then motioned for me to follow him. He led me to the fireplace - there was a shelf around the outside of it and on the shelf were various cuts of beef. I selected three long narrow cuts that appeared to be beef tenderloin - cut with the grain (we cut the piece of meat across the grain - wrap it with bacon and call it filet migon). The chef picked up the cuts, smiled and nodded his approval and asked "Que" I said - dos - media - un -burned. He laughed and said "Bueno".

When I returned to the table Frank and Jim were already drinking wine and eating pan (bread). I joined them and said - "Were all set - and I think this is really going to be a treat." It was. The salad contained lettuce, spinach, tomatoes, olives and was seasoned with oil and vinegar - the tenderloin steaks were tender and succulent - and the potatoes had been cut in chunks (cubed) - brushed with olive oil - seasoned, and cooked over the fire. This was truly the best meal we had in Europe - and it cost about $3(U.S.). Frank said "Bill, I didn't know you spoke Spanish - but you sure did good." I said - "De nada."

I'll be the first to admit that I got very homesick - particularly at night. I missed my wife and new son something fierce. I wrote a letter every night and made 2 phone calls a month. (at $40 per call - I could not afford more). Caro wrote every day and at least once a week a letter contained a picture of Michael.

There was a library at the Officers Club so I did a lot of reading. I usually checked out books and read in my room. After I got the high fidelity set I played music as I read.

The only other thing to do was go to the Officers Club and drink, gossip, play pool, or play cards. A few times they had "live" entertainment for us - I remember one group in particular - Les Brown and his band of Renown. there were great.

CHAPTER 19

ANYONE FOR BRIDGE

One night I was already in my pajamas and lying in my bunk - deeply immersed in a good book when there was a rap on my door. I went to the door and opened it - there stood Frank. Frank said, "Get dressed Tommy and let's go to the club and play some bridge. I told him I would rather read but he was persistent. He said "I've found a couple of pigeons who want to play for a penny a point."

I couldn't imagine who he had found - we were good bridge players and had beat everyone on the base - no one would play us for money anymore. I asked "Who have you found that think they can beat us?" Frank said "A couple of old retired British army officers."

It sounded like it might be entertaining so I got us, got dressed, and accompanied Frank to the Officers Club. We went in and Frank led the way to a card table in the corner. Two distinguished looking old gentlemen were seated at the table and they rose and introduced themselves - both were retired Colonels from the Queens Army.

We sat down and began playing bridge - Frank and I vs. the British. We won the first few hands and a crowd began to gather to watch the game. In hindsight, I think the British let us win so we would become over confident for thereafter the hands we won were down few and far between. The British Colonels had literally been statewide all over the world. Their last assignment has been India. They had played bridge together hundreds, if not thousands, of times and it appeared they could almost read each other's mind. Again in hindsight, I am sure they had some "secret" way they could signal one another - perhaps by the stories they told. I know for sure that by midnight, they has thoroughly whipped our butts and it cost each of us about $125.

On the way back to the B.O.Q. Frank apologized and I said "Next, time, be more careful of the pigeons you select."

CHAPTER 20

SKIP BOUGHT THE FARM

One night when I went to the Officers Club for supper I heard someone yell "Bill - over here." I looked and saw a friend who had been in navigation class with me - Skip Oakley. I walked over to the table and we did a bear hug and Skip introduced me to the man seated at the table with him - a major Hines. I joined them for supper and learned they had landed their F-94C the night before, spent the night at the B.O.Q., and would take off at 10 a.m.

When I asked Skip what they were up to his explanation was "I can't talk about it." I figured he was telling me - I can't discuss it in front of Major Hines, the pilot, or that it was none of my business. Either way, I didn't pursue the subject.

We had a nice leisurely breakfast and a long visit. We each told of our Air Force experiences, families, fellow classmates, etc. Skip had finished training and been assigned to the Air Defense Command and rode the back seat in the F-94 (a hot all weather interceptor).

Like me, he had married a Texas girl and they had a little daughter, about 6 months old. His assignment was Otis AFB, Barnstable Co., Mass (Cape Cod area). His family just loved the area. Major Hines said his family did also - particularly his teen age son.

It was nearing 9:00 a.m. and Major Hines was getting antsy so I told them I would go to the flight line with them and see them off. I located a fellow officer who had a jeep parked outside and got him to drive us to the flight line.

Skip took great pride in showing me the F-94. It was one hot airplane and I admit some jealousy. They said when the afterburner kicked in they could fly almost straight up and got to 50,000 feet in seconds.

After they completed their pre-flight check list they climbed aboard and got strapped in - then fired her up. What a terrific noise it made. I waved as they taxied out to the main runway and watched as they started their take off roll and picked up speed.

But something didn't look right. The runway was 10,000 foot long and they had used about 3/4 of it and had not become airborne (I figured they would have broken contact at no more than 5000 ft.).

Something was indeed wrong. The aircraft never got more than 15 to 20 feet high and flew straight as an arrow right into a cluster of three large trees about a mile from the end of the runway. I watched in horror as it hit the trees, exploded, and burst into flames. A couple of fire trucks went racing to the crash site. By the time they put out the fire, there was not much left - only ashes.

I didn't know what happened to the F-94 - all I knew was that my friend skip had "bought the farm."

I went back to the B.O.Q. and told Frank and Jim what had happened. They tried to comfort me and Frank got a bottle of Crown Royal and I gulped down a glass full. Thank goodness - we weren't scheduled to fly until the next day.

Later in the day a couple of Colonels came to my room and quizzed me. They were conducting an investigation of the crash. I told them everything I knew and agreed not to discuss it with anyone until now.

CHAPTER 21

OFF DUTY IN EUROPE

Some of the time we were like firemen while stationed in England - three days on duty then three days off. During the days off I rode my motorcycle all over the British isles - England, Scotland, Ireland, and Wales. The countryside was just beautiful - so manicured. It seemed as if each foot of land had a greens keeper. I always wore civilian clothes when I traveled but the British knew I was yank the minute I opened my mouth. Although somewhat reserved, they were nevertheless friendly. Jim and I usually traveled together but sometimes I went alone.

Frank had warned us that the young women would be forward sometimes - in England and all over Europe. Most of them wanted to marry a yank and come to the United States. Further, there was a severe shortage of men in Europe in those days - many were killed during World War II. Because of my strict puritanical upbringing and the fact that I was a relatively newly married man - I shed away from the women. There were many opportunities but I always passed them by, Jim was the same; we were among the few who wore our wedding rings.

I remember stopping at a place called "Woburn castle". During the guided tour this sweet young thing kept pressing up against me. She was very beautiful.

After the tour, we had tea and crumpets and she cornered me and we carried on a conversation. According to her, she was from a very wealthy family and was staying at their family summer estate - not far from there. She invited me to come and spend the evening with her - and made sure that I understood that she meant that literally. She asked me to sleep with her - in her bed. I declined - got on my motorcycle and roared away. Scouts honor - "I did".

On another trip Jim and I went to Bournemouth - we got a room at a "roadhouse" there, changed into bathing suits, and went to the beach. Before we realized it, we were surrounded by a bevy of British beauties. They all wanted to go to our room and fool around - taking turns. There must have been a dozen of them. Again we declined.

On every trip - we returned to the base with our saddle bags loaded with stuff. We couldn't resist the bargains - everything was less expensive than in the states. Yep - we took lots of pictures and bought lots of stuff - Irish linens, scotch whiskey, wool suits, sturdy leather shoes, china, silver, etc. One of our discoveries were the pawnshops. There were owned by the Government and loaded with silver, china, etc. We were told that much of their inventory had been obtained by "confiscation" (for unpaid taxes).

Another neat way to travel was on U.S. Air Force courier flights and mail flights. We had planes flying all over Europe - all the time. They selected passengers by rank - the highest ranking officers got top priority - on down the

pecking order. Poor enlisted men didn't have much of a chance. Since we were in civilian clothes, I would always sign the waiting list as Captain Bill Thomas, aide to General Trump. It worked every time.

On of my first trips on a courier plane was to Wiesbaden, Germany. They had the best stocked P.X. (post exchange) there that I ever saw - before or after. I really went on a real shopping binge buying hummel figurines, black forest clocks (cuckoo clocks), records, and my prized possession - a Telefunken high fidelity set with an am/fm radio and a short wave radio. After I purchased the telefuken - it struck me that I had no means to carry it back to England. I asked the sales lady if she had any suggestions. She asked "Where are you stationed?" I told her "Greenham Common AFB, Newbury, England." She said - "We can ship it to the base exchange at Greenham Common - it should arrive by next Wednesday." I said - "That's perfect." (and it did - the BX even delivered it to my room the following Wednesday.)

Some of the other memorable trips I took on courier planes included (A) Copenhagen, (B) Paris, (C) Madrid, and finally - a full week in Rome (combination courier plane and train).

Jim and I caught a courier plane at Brize Norten and flew to Copenhagen. When we landed, we hired a cab to take us on a guided tour of the city. We took pictures of the statues, museums, etc. We had lunch in a nice restaurant in the downtown area. Before we finished lunch, five gorgeous Scandinavian blondes had invited themselves to join us for lunch. They mostly drank beer while we ate. Two of them spoke English (our driver also spoke some English - he was having a ball) and acted as interpreters. They even picked up the tab for our lunch. There were perhaps 40 people in this restaurant/bar - two old men, us, and the rest were beautiful young women.

After lunch, our driver took us to what he described as a very special place - and it was that. it was the beach. Most of the young women there were bare naked. I have never before or since seen so many good looking naked women on display. What a visual treat. Viva Scandinavia. We couldn't touch so we looked extra hard. The temptation was almost overpowering - but again we did not yield. (Caro - I hope you take note of this).

We spent the night in a downtown hotel. The next morning our driver came by and took us on a tour of the countryside - then we returned to the airport and caught a commercial flight back to London and the train to the base.

The weekend I went to Paris - I went alone. I caught a courier plane in London and flew to Orly airport in Paris. There I hired a cab for a guided tour of Paris. We went to all the usual tourist spots - Eifel tower, Follies Bejure, artist colony along the Seine, and finally dinner at Coco's. If prices were inexpensive elsewhere in Europe - Paris made up for it. I started with about $400 in my wallet - and after paying for dinner - I was broke. My driver took me back to the airport where I drank coffee, smoked, and finally caught a plane back to London at 4am Sunday morning. I had a bad taste in my mouth about Paris (and France) - still do. the French were unfriendly and downright rude.

This brings up a point that disturbs me. Why does the U.S.A. always stick its long nose into problems all over the world. In my opinion, we have wasted zillions of dollars and untold lives over the years "saving" foreign countries. It has been my experience that they certainly don't appreciate it - most of them <u>hate us</u> and think we are dumb.

Frank joined us for the trip to Madrid. He had never been there (and I think he remembered the steak dinner at Zaragoza). We rode the train from Newbury to London and caught a courier flight to Madrid. As usual, we found a cab driver that spoke a little English and hired him to show us the sights. At every stop - we took pictures - and usually bought something.

The highpoint of this trip was the bullfights on Sunday afternoon. Why people can get so excited over some one sticking a bull in the butt with darts then killing him by plunging a sword into his heart I'll never understand. But of course, they don't understand how we can get so excited watching football - where helmeted men line up and try to knock heck out of one another. People are weird the world over I suppose - just a different kind of weird. As Dandy Don (Meredith) so aptly put it - "Different strokes for different folks."

We did find a great restaurant in Madrid and enjoyed another excellent steak dinner.

I took a few days of leave to make the trip to Rome. I was not able to catch a flight to Rome but did catch a ride across the English channel to Amsterdam. In Amsterdam, I found what was, I suppose, a travel agent, who helped me book passage on trains through to Rome. I rode through Belgian, parts of France and Germany, Austria, then Italy. The most interesting thing about this trip was the different languages encountered and the different currencies - extremely confusing for a country boy - but also very educational. I decided to wear my uniform on this trip - and that was, in hindsight, a mistake. I also started the trip with American Express travelers checks and British pounds. I ate most of my meals on the train and whenever I had to change trains, I would usually take a few hours for a quick sightseeing side trip and picture taking expedition. At one such stop (I think it was Strasburg, France) there was a large crowd gathered around a bearded man standing on a box and making a speech. I walked up to the crowd and people spat at me - some threw rocks. I quickly retreated and was later told by a person who witnessed the incident, that the speech maker was a local communist official who was stirring up the crowd.

At another stop (I believe this was at Milano, Italy), there was a street vendor selling peaches from a cart. I stopped and selected a couple of peaches - and handed him a British pound note. He ran off down the street - shouting something and waving the pound note. I ate a peach and stood there. In a few minutes, the vendor returned with a big smile on his face and carrying a paper sack. He jabbered something and handed the sack to me - it was full of Italian Lyra - <u>my</u> <u>change</u>! Their currency was practically worthless.

When we arrived in Rome I was again spat upon by the Romans. I decided that I had best get a room and change to civilian clothes as quickly as possible. I caught a cab and went to the hotel that the "travel agent" in Amsterdam had hopefully made reservations in. After much searching and scrambling - the clerk finally gave me a room after I rolled a silver dollar across the counter to him. (Somewhere on the trip I had gotten the silver dollar when I had cashed a travelers check). When I crossed the lobby to the elevator, I passed a gorgeous brunette who was sitting in the lobby. She smiled and I returned a smile. When I stepped on the elevator - she was right behind me. When I arrived at my floor and stepped off - she stepped off. I found my room and opened the door - I stepped in the room and she was right behind me. I told her to leave. She smiled and spoke to me in Italian. Obviously, we could not communicate. I made a motion in sign language which I thought represented - <u>get</u> <u>the</u> <u>heck</u> <u>out</u> <u>of</u> <u>here</u>. She responded in sign language indicating what she had in mind. She next grabbed my B-4 bag and started unloading my clothes - hanging them in the closet and placing them in a chest. Then, she turned back the bed and went into the bathroom. Next, she stepped out of the bathroom - naked as a jay bird - but a heck of a lot prettier. She looked like Gina Lollibraida. My Lord - what temptations. But again I declined. I had a heck of a time getting her to dress and leave - but she finally did. Honest injun.

The concierge at the hotel spoke fluent English. I told her I would be in Rome four days and wanted to see as much as I could while I was there. I explained I was in the Air Force - stationed in England. I also said I wanted to attend a papal audience, if possible. She took charge of my four days and did an excellent job. I joined some professional guided tours for two days and saw most of the usual tourist sports - Fontana De Trevi, Parthenon, St. Lukes, The Vatican, the War Memorial, Seven Hills of Rome, etc. Next, a private tourist guide took over and we spent a full day at the summer residence of the Pope - Castle Gondalfo. There were thousands of people there from all over the world. Dozens of concessions stands dispensed food, lemonade, soft drinks, prayer beads, religious medals, prayers, etc. - All allegedly "Blessed by La Papa - the Pope." The Swiss Guards guarded the gate to the castle but at 1:00 pm opened the gates to the courtyard. It was like a cattle stamped as thousands poured into the courtyard and became packed like sardines. I was nearly trampled by about 20 large Africans that looked like Zulu warriors. The Pope (Pope Paul XXII) finally appeared on the balcony and addressed the audience in about six languages.

There was a constant chat from the crowd - Vily La Papa! Viva La Papa! the Pope finally retired and the crowd dispersed - just in time for me - I was almost crushed. It amazed me - the power the Pope had over this audience.

My last day in Rome was spent off the beaten path - we went outside the city and stopped at a winery, saw the old aqueduct (that brought water to ancient Rome from the mountains, and ended the day in a quaint little restaurant outside Rome that was owned and operated by an American - from Brooklyn. I met him and we sipped wine as his chef prepared some veal dish for us - it was great. (My third best meal in Europe - Spain was best). He asked all sorts of questions about what was going on in the U.S.A. - it seems he had been a G.I. who married a girl from Rome during World War II. She "forced" him to move to Rome - at least that was his story.

The next day I was able to catch a ride on a courier plane back to London - and back to flying and earning a living.

CHAPTER 22

TIRED OF BEING FOLKED ABOUT

In reading what I've written so far - I discovered that I had omitted the most popular destination of our weekend trips - London. Nor have I written much about Newbury. There was a race track (horse racing) and I spent many afternoons there - buying hay for the race horses.

We could catch a train in Newbury and be in London in about one hour. If we had no plans for the weekend - we would usually go to London - to see a show and eat if nothing else. After the first trip when you took in Buckingham Palace, London Bridge, Piccadilly Circus, Parliament, etc. - there weren't many other places to go.

There were a couple of amusing incidents on these trips to London.

Once, we were at the train station in Newbury, standing on the platform, waiting for the train to London. When it arrived at the station ,it was raining and the train engineer and the tender were absolutely soaked. I asked a brit who was standing nearby - "Why don't they enclose the cabs on the train engines." His prompt and proper British response was "In England, that just isn't done."

The trains quit running at midnight so if you missed the last train out of London - you were "Up the creek" so to speak. If you had to fly the next day - big trouble.

For some reason long forgotten, Frank, Jim and I went to London one Sunday. We were scheduled to fly early Monday morning. We probably went to a pub and late that afternoon went to a restaurant we had located that served relatively good food (compared to the base at least) Frank had bought a London newspaper and commented - there is a play at the Bijou Theatre I've always wanted to see - it's called "Anastasia." We said, lets finish eating and go to the play.

When we arrived at the theatre, the performance had already started and it was sold out. There was a late performance starting at 10 p.m. We bought tickets for the late performance and retired to a neighborhood bar and proceeded to do a little drinking (even bought a bottle for the road).

We went to the play and enjoyed it - it was about the family of the Russian Czar. I think Vanessa Redgrave starred in it but am not sure. When the play was over and we got back on the street Frank said "It late - we better hurry to the depot or we will miss the train." I said "Too late to worry about the train - it's 12:30."

So we stopped at the nearest bar and had another drink to discuss how the heck we were going to get back to the base in time to meet our scheduled takeoff. The bartender was no help - he said all the cabbies went home at midnight too. An old Scotsman was sitting at a table near us. He spoke up and said "I think I know a cabbie who might still be around at this hour." We asked "Who". He told us that Angus McTavish usually operated his hack over by the docks on the river Thames until 2 a.m. - he picked up ship's crew members and took them to lodging, etc. He drew us a map on a napkin on how to get there. It was a 10 or 12 block walk but we had no choice. We paid for his drinks, thanked him, and started walking.

Sure enough, we found an ancient cab parked under a street light. As we approached it, an ancient head of an ancient man peered out the window by the driver's seat. We asked him if his cab was for hire. He said "Yes" so we crawled into the back seat. He asked "Destination?" We said "Greenham Common AFB." He asked "Where is it located?" We said "Newbury." He didn't know where Newbury was located either so I carefully explained it was 80 kilometers due west of London – toward Plymouth. He finally thought he could find the place. But he had another problem – he was low on petrol and all the stations were closed. By now we were practically begging him to take us to Greenham Common and had offered him 25 pounds for the trip. Jim asked "Are there any tankers docked on the river." Yes, he remembered picking up a tanker crew Saturday night. So, we drove down the docks and found the tankers. Jim got out and approached the tanker and yelled out in his deep Kansas voice "Anybody home" – a light came on in the pilot house and a head popped out paying "Blimey – what is bloody (bad, bad word) heck is going on?" Jim responded – "Got an emergency – must have some gasoline." He moved forward and met the sailor – they talked and Jim gave him something (money of course) – in a few minutes the sailor returned with a bucket (about 5 gallons) of gasoline (petrol) which Jim poured into the hack. We gave the sailor a swig from our whiskey bottle and took one our self. Soon we were leaving London and were put putting through the Countryside.

We were feeling pretty good now that our transportation problem was solved. We continued to pass the bottle around and then started telling dirty jokes. We also discussed England and complained about the food, weather, trains that stopped at midnight, worn out hacks, etc, etc. In truth - we had become drunk and disorderly - D & D.

We felt the old hack starting to slow and heard the squealing sound as angus applied the brakes he pulled off the pavement, came to a complete stop, exited the cab, opened the back door and said "Out – everybody out." We stumbled out and he started to get back in the cab. We asked "What's going on – what's the matter?"

His response was "I'm tired of being folked about by you yanks."

Again, we told him we were sorry and pleaded with him to take us to our base. It was not until we raised the ante to 35 pounds that he agreed to complete the journey. We meekly crawled back into his cab and not another word was spoken until we finally arrived at the front gate of Greenham Common. We got out of the cab and gave angus 40 pounds (1 pound = $2.80 U.S. at that time). He didn't say Thank You, kiss my British butt, or nothing – just got into his hack and left.

It was past 4:00 a.m. in the morning and the enlisted man at the gate almost didn't let us in – even after he examined our ID cards. He finally did but had no transportation for us. So we started walking to the squadron OPS building. There was an O.D. (Officer of the Day) on duty and he had a pot of coffee made and some French pastries which he shared with us. We got into our flying suits, put on our boots, got our helmets, brief case, and parachute and went to the plane. It was 5:30 am. By 6:00 am preflight was complete and we had the six G.E. jets fired up. We taxied to the active runway - got takeoff clearance - and at 6:00 am - "Off we go - into the wild blue yonder." The only thing that saved us on that mission was we stayed on 100% oxygen and Frank remembered to bring his thermos of steaming black coffee. We had forgotten the flight lunches.

When we landed that afternoon we were some whipped puppies. We went straight to the BOQ and hit the sack. I awoke about midnight - Frank and Jim were talking and had a pot of coffee brewing. I got up, took a shower, and care back and heated some canned chili. We ate chili and crackers and drank coffee. I turned on the F.M. radio and located a station in Germany that was playing good music. We were almost back to normal. We laughed a lot, recounting our adventure of the night before. The only thing we had scheduled for Tuesday was to plan the mission for Wednesday. We agreed to get together about 3 pm Tuesday for mission planning.

Frank returned to his room and Jim crawled back in the sack - soon he was snoring. I lay down but couldn't go back to sleep. I wrote Caro a letter and lay back down and switched the short wave on the Telefunken - I listened to some maritime communications for awhile (you could pick up everything in Europe on that telefunken - Germa, French, Spanish, Scandinavian, Russian, and English.

I picked up a paperback and started reading - soon I dropped off to sleep. At five a.m. I was wide awake again. I have never been able to sleep late in the morning when the sun comes up - I'm awake. By the same token - when it gets dark I get sleepy. Jim was still making Z's and I knew Frank would be too - I knew both would sleep till noon at least.

I got up and got dressed. I rode my motorcycle to the Officers Club and had juice, English muffins, oatmeal, and coffee. (at least they could cook oatmeal). There were only a couple of other guys up and about this early. I was bored - couldn't really think of anything to do this fine morning. I called Caro and talked to her my allotted $40 worth. She was lonely and wanted me home. I told her we only had two more weeks to go.

I crawled back on the Royal Enfield and rode back to the B.O.Q. There were a couple of guys playing golf. Then it hit me - Golf! I had won a set of golf clubs in a poker game the first month at Greenham Common. One of the pilots in our squadron (Captain Musterman) had been a club pro before he was recalled and I had played a couple of rounds with him. However, I could not crank up my old baseball swing and he had given up on teaching me how to play golf and I had about given up on learning the game.

However, this was one of the very few sunshiny days we had seen since we came to England and I felt like being outside. When I got to the B.O.Q. I parked the bike and went to my room and got my golf clubs. I carried them to the tee box at #1 hole - which was close to the B.O.Q. - the #3 tee box was right behind the B.O.Q. Even though the golf course was located on the base, for public relations purposes, the British from Newbury were allowed to play on it.

About the time I arrived at #1 this small frail looking British lady rode up on her bicycle. She had a small golf bag on her shoulder that couldn't have contained more than six clubs. She introduced herself - Mrs. Molly Pembroke - widow. Her husband had been killed in World War II. I judged her to be about 50 years old and to weigh about 90 pounds. I introduced myself she asked if she would join me for a "round of golf." I told her that I really didn't know how to play and had intended to play by myself and just practice - didn't even intend to keep score.

She scolded me and said "Lieutenant, if you are going to do something - you may as well learn to do it right" (I also learned she was a school teacher). She offered to teach me the game of golf and point out my mistakes. I agreed so we started a round of golf.

Molly (we soon were calling each other "Molly" and "William") teed up her British ball (which was smaller than the U.S. balls), selected a wood (she only carried one - a 3 wood) from her bag, and hit it straight as an arrow down the fairway. The first 100 yards of each hole was not mowed - it was grass about 6" high, with a path mowed down the center. Also, the mowed fairways were narrow and the greens were small. Molly's ball sailed over the tall grass and rolled about 25 yards up the mowed fairway - in line with the path.

It was my turn. I teed up my ball, selected the driver, and took my homerun baseball cut at it. The ball went about 200 yards and did the usual banana arc to the right and sliced deep into the rough. Molly didn't say a word - just walked to her ball, selected an iron, and pinged it another 100 yards - straight down the fairway. I then waded out into the right rough to the area where I had last seen my ball. The rough was thick and lush - all that rain. I never did find my ball but I found 3 other balls - 2 of them British.

I walked back to the fairway, found a nice little hump of grass, carefully placed a ball on it so that it was sitting up nicely. I pulled out a 4 iron and took another home run swing at the ball. Again - the old banana slice - 150 yards forward and 50 yards to the right into deep rough. I started toward my ball as Molly addresses her ball and pinged it another 125 yards - straight down the middle. After wading around in the rough for another ten minutes, I gave up on finding my ball and walked back to the fairway. I found another nice hump of grass to hit off of and placed one of the British balls on it. This time I selected a 3 iron and took a mighty swing at it - this one didn't slice so bad - it just went sailing about 50 yards over the green.

As I walked toward my ball, Molly pulled out a wedge and pinged her ball to about 5 feet of the cup. I found my ball, pulled out my wedge, and hit it back over the green and into a sand trap. It took me three more shots to get out of the sand and on the green - then I four putted of course - Molly sank her put.

We walked to the #2 tee box and when we got there, Molly pulled out a score card and said "What was your score Lieutenant." I quickly added the times I remembered hitting the ball - subtracted a couple - and glibly said "Seven". She didn't write it down - rather she described how I had played the hole and said - "I make your score thirteen" I said "No - fourteen, I lost a ball." She smiled and wrote down 14 for me and 4 for herself.

She teed up her ball and his another one about 150 yards - straight down the middle. I then teed up my ball but before I hit it I said "Molly, would you mind teaching me how to play golf." She just beamed as she said "I would be delighted." She said, I think you have the natural talent for the game and will make a good golfer. She then went into an explanation and demonstration of the golf swing. She made me take a 6 iron and practice several swings - critiquing me after each swing. Once I got it through my head to use my left arm and hand for the basic swing - the swing started to improve. Next she explained the importance of striking the ball on the correct spot on the club face - the sweet spot.

Before I hit the ball she said - don't swing very hard - just concentrate on hitting the ball straight, when you master that - you can then start working on distance. Finally, she let me hit my ball and sure enough - it went straight down the middle - about 15 yards past her ball. She smiled and said "You hit that one on the sweet spot sir."

There were only a couple of foursomes on the course so we played at a very leisurely pace and let them play through. Molly instructed me on every shot. Occasionally I would over swing and hit another slice. When I did, she made me hit another ball - softly. We both looked for my balls in the rough and found several others.

By the time we made the turn she was writing down <u>legitimate</u> scores of Molly - 5; Bill 7 - I still couldn't putt. It was noon and we were near the officers club - I invited her to lunch. She accepted so we stopped for a sandwich, chips and coke. Then we played the back nine which brought us back near her bicycle and the B.O.Q. We exchanged phone numbers and agreed to play more golf when we could get away at the same time. (Several times I had phone messages from "Molly" and Frank and Jim thought I had a girlfriend - I did - we became good friends as well as golf partners). By the time we left England I was regularly breaking 90 - Molly was a terrific golf instructor.

The wing had a golf tournament the last week we were in England and I had the second low net score (playing with an 18 handicap).

CHAPTER 23

RETURN TO KANSAS

The day finally arrived for our return home – to Kansas. I think everyone was homesick and ready to leave England. We left with much more than we brought over. We loaded our possessions" in the bomb bay of the B-47 (except for a case of Champaign which we loaded in the pressurized cockpit. Frank had sold his car and Jim had sold his motorcycle – but I kept mine. The people at the B.X. had packed all the China, crystal, etc. in wooden boxes – packed in straw. We also carried some of the squadron stuff and some of the enlisted men's stuff in our plane. Our bomb bay was packed fuel of stuff.

The flight back to Kansas was uneventful. We were about the third aircraft to take off and the third to land at Smokey Hill. Our families were there to meet us – it was great to be "home". Caro and I embraced and jumped in the Chevy and headed straight home – and to bed. I rented a trailer next day and went to the base to pick up all my stuff – it was a trailer full. Caro was very pleased with all the quality things I had bought – hi/fi, china, sterling, linens, cashmeres, etc., etc. – she didn't think much of my royal Enfield (motorcycle) however.

For the next few days we never stopped talking – me telling Caro of all my experiences – (most of which are covered in this book) and she telling me of all she had done while I was away. She had met a lot of new people and learned much about Salina and the surrounding area. For example, "Did I know that the movie PICNIC had been filmed in Salina? Did I know there was a Swedish community (Lindsburg) near Salina that had neat crafts? Did I know there was a famous stage coach stop (Ellsworth) west of Salina that served great fried chicken? etc. etc. It became obvious that she had accepted Salina and had come to like it.

Flying had settled down to a routine. We were old experienced heads and highly qualified – one of the top crews in the wing. We took pride in our work.

At the end of three months – it was time to "rotate" back to England. This time – I wasn't that excited about the trip overseas. Kansas and home was better.

CHAPTER 24

HUNTING AND FISHING IN KANSAS

I have always found a way to get in some hunting and fishing - no matter where I was. Air Force duty in Kansas was no different.

One of the first places I visited in Salina was the Purina Feed Store. I got to know the owners and would "hand out" there and meet the farmers who came to buy feed and seed. Almost every one of them gave me permission to hunt on their property - especially when I told them I would shoot the Jack Rabbits and Coyotes.

One day when I was loafing at the feed store, a farmer came in and was trying to sell several guns. I bought a .22 Stevens rifle and a 12 gauge Remington pump. Also got permission to hunt on his place.

My hunting buddy was the base dentist, Captain Harris ("Doc") from Michigan who I met at a dental visit. He and his family (wife and 2 daughters) lived about 2 blocks from me.

Both of us loved outdoor activities – especially hunting and fishing. It was the fall of the year and our first couple of trips were fishing trips to Lake Kannapolis. We caught enough fish to put on a neighborhood fish fry.

Next, dove season opened and we went dove hunting in the flint hills south of town. We located a "gap" in the ridge and concealed ourselves on the back side of the gap and blasted away at the migrating doves that flew through it.

Our next adventure was pheasant hunting. There was a large area of government owned land on the northwest side of the base that we were allowed to hunt on. It was surrounded by wheat fields and contained many pheasants. The problem was trying to get close enough to them to get them to fly. Jim and I finally worked out a system where one would drive (trail) the bird and the other would circle around and head it off. Those pheasant were mighty good eating.

Finally, the snow came and our hunting was limited to jackrabbits and coyotes. All the farmers would allow us to hunt them. We would trudge across fields – hoping to jump a rabbit or coyote. Sometimes, you could see a jackrabbits earns sticking out of the snow – in which you tried to get close enough for a shot. Usually, one of us carried a rifle (me normally) and the other –a shotgun.

One day, we stopped at a farm and asked permission to hunt – the farmer said "sure" I saw a coyote out back of the barn just a few minutes ago". Jim looked and said "there he goes across that field." We jumped into the Chevy and took out in pursuit (I had chains on it). We were going down a fence line about 40 mph when the bottom fell out and all we could see was snow. We had hit a low spot where the snow had drifted and literally buried the car in the snow drift. The farmer tried to tug the car out with his farm tractor – but couldn't. We finally located a wrecker service with a winch truck who agreed to come out and extract the Chevy – but that took the rest of the day and our hunt was over. At least we learned to stay on roads after that.

A few hunters would be positioned in a line at the end of a field of wheat stubble. the other hunters would form a line at the other end of the field and would walk down the field -  pushing the pheasants in front of them. Some of them would fly and hunters would yell either rooster or hen. Many shots would follow "Rooster" but none following "Hen" - they were protected. (That is not entirely accurate - a few hens were also accidentally shot). Paul's mother prepared a huge pheasant dinner for us - it was a great hunt.

We also got to deer hunt one time. The farmer who I bought the guns from leased some land in Coffee County and he said it had a few deer on it. He gave up permission to go deer hunting on it. Doc has a 30-06 rifle that he had borrowed from someone but I only had the .12 gauge shotgun and Buckshot. There was snow on the ground and although I saw a fern deer, I could never get into shooting range. Doc got a nice 6 point  Buck.

There are hunting and fishing possibilities everywhere - you just have to root them out.

CHAPTER 25

SAD DAY AT SMOKEY HILL

After our second rotation to England and return to Kansas we were scheduled for complete physical exams. Jim and I passed just fine but Frank didn't – he had high blood pressure and an erratic E.C.G. He was taken off flight status and given a desk job. What a sad, sad day. At first, Jim and I feared we would be split up and transferred. But that didn't happen. An aircraft commander was instead, transferred to our squadron and assigned to our crew – 1st Lt. Gene Rosselot.

We liked Gene and he was a good pilot – but things just weren't the same. No one could have replaced Frank in our minds. He was the best.

It took us a few missions before we got used to each other and functioning as a team. Gene was a little high strung and tended to get over excited at times – but Jim had a settling effect on him. We maintained our proficiency and lead crew status (L-92) and one of the best crews in the squadron.

As proof of our proficiency – we were "promoted" to "test" crew status. At the time, we thought this was great – just imagine – these 1st Lieutenants – a test crew for the mighty B-47. Heck, almost all the other crews on the base had at least one Colonel – and they weren't "test" crew status. (little did we know).

One day they told us we were going to do some conventional bombing – using the optic (Norden) bomb sight. (In hindsight – they were considering using the B-47's in the Korean and later Vietnam wars). A bomb range had been set up south of the field – on the edge of the government property. The target was a bulls eye painted on the ground. They rigged a bomb rack in the bomb bay of our B-47 and loaded it with 200 pound "blue darters" – old bomb cases with a light powder charge in them so you could see where they hit.

We took off and made our bomb runs at the target – from 39,000 ft. we made ten bomb runs and dropped 10 blue darters – and hit the target one time – the other missed by 1000 to 3000 ft. Not too impressive – you could kill a lot of friendly troops with that inaccuracy.

Other crews then tried their luck at this target But instead of killing people – they slaughtered chickens. There was a chicken farm that joined the base - right across the property line where the bombing range had been placed. There is no telling how many chickens were allegedly killed by those erratic blue darters. All I know is that got to be a standing joke at the base. "What are you going to do this trip?" Answer – "Bomb them chickens."

CHAPTER 26

ADIOS SAC – HELLO TEXAS

My tour of active duty was rapidly drawing near - between Christmas and New Year. We didn't talk about it much but I knew that Gene and Jim really wanted me to stay on active duty and keep the crew intact. Col. Hempleman had called me to his office a couple of times to chat - sort of father - son type of chats. He was doing his best to convince me to make a career of the Air Force - he was confident I could ultimately advance to the rank of Colonel - and maybe even General. The most attractive argument though was retirement after 20 years - I would be able to <u>retire</u> before age 45.

All the other ROTC type officers in the squadron had re-enlisted for another four years - I was the only hold out. Next, Colonel Low called me to his office and gave me his sales pitch - plus, he told me the Air Force had invested $500,000 in me and it was my "duty" to stay in. (I didn't buy this argument).

I asked if I could get transferred to a B-58 squadron. The B-58 was the latest bomber - and it was "Hot." (Super Sonic).

He made a phone call - hung up - and told me. No. The Air Force only has a few B-58's and they are crewing them with only very experienced pilots and observers.

Meanwhile, back at the home front - Caro was putting even more pressure on me to get out and get on with my career in Public Accounting. I was officially on Military leave of absence from one of the big 8 accounting firms. Further, she was fearful of me getting killed. And finally, she was pregnant again - and homesick.

About mid-October, we had a squadron meeting. When we got to the meeting, there was a lot of brass there from SAC headquarters (Offutt AFB, Omaha). Colonel Hempleman introducing the officers from SAC headquarters - and one by one they made their speeches to us. The first officer to address us was from intelligence. He told us of the rapid strides the Russians had made in aircraft technology, radar, and missiles - especially missiles. He explained that, under the present circumstances, our chances of getting our targets was less than 50%. He spoke with a tone of urgency.

The next officer basically repeated the story and enforced it with a movie and slides of the new Russian missiles - including huge intercontinental ballistic missiles.

He was followed by still another officer with a slide show that showed us some of the new U.S. Technology and weapons - including ICBM's. He said in the near future, the missiles would replace the bombers.

The final speaker was a general who said that SAC had come up with a way to defeat the missiles and that we would immediately start training for low altitude penetration and bombing. He explained the two new low altitude maneuvers which S.A.C. had developed - the "pop us" maneuver and the labs (low altitude bombing system) maneuver.

For the "pop up" maneuver, the B-47 was flown on the deck (tree top level) to the target - then a rapid pull up (climb) to 18,000 feet was initiated. At the top of the maneuver, the bomb was released, after which the aircraft was quickly rolled out and dived back to the deck.

For the labs maneuver, the B-47 was flown through an immelmann. The airplane was flown on the deck to the target, then pulled up in a half loop. At the top of the loop, the bomb was released, and a half roll was initiated for "escape" from the impending nuclear explosion. He then showed a film which demonstrated these maneuvers.

There followed a question and answer period. Most of us were concerned with two things -

(a) Was the B-47 strong enough for these maneuvers, and

(b) How the heck could we get away from the nuclear blast if we were on the deck.

The headquarters boys assured us - "no sweat".

After they completed their dog and pony show, Col. Hempleman stood up and said "Will all the test crews stay seated - everyone else is dismissed."

There were three lonely crews sitting in that room after everyone cleared out. Colonel Hempleman told us what we already knew - we would be the first to try out this wild and crazy stuff. He told us we would start ground school immediately and the pilots would have a couple of days in the simulator before we actually flew a mission.

The following week, all three test crews were aboard their planes and we took off one by one for a little low altitude bombing.

We flew to a relatively uninhabited area of western Kansas. We had drawn straws before we took off and we were the first to do a "pop up" and third to do a "labs." All three aircraft were in a lazy 360 turn at about 25,000 feet - getting up our nerve. Finally Gene said "Grab your tail boys - here goes" as we dived to the deck - just above the wheat fields. We went ripping across the country side and pulled up in a steep climb - I was watching the altimeter and could feel it when Gene was getting set to roll out - he said "release" and I already had my hand on the bomb release and "released" - we rolled out and dived. The plane shuddered a bit and the "G" forces were much greater than we had anticipated. Otherwise, "no sweat".

Gene got on the radio and said "Ok Art - your turn - that was fun!" Capt Art Shaw came back on the radio "Yeah, I bet it was - I watched." We were climbing back up and leveled out at 10,000 ft and watched Art and his crew do a "pop up". it really was kind of neat. They climbed up to 10,000 ft and joined us and Art said (on the radio) - "OK you Mexican Steve Canyon - let's see what you learned." Captain Julio Martinez said "Hi Ho Silver" and dived his B-47 to the deck. We watched him pop up then he came over and joined us. We flew around for a few minutes while the aircraft commanders talked on the radio - discussing the recently completed pop up maneuver, condition of the B-47's , the upcoming labs maneuver, etc. Finally, Captain Martinez said "Well, guess it's my turn to show you boys how to do the labs maneuver." We watched as he nosed his B-47 over and dived toward the wheat fields below - we flew along over him as he skimmed across the fields then started his climb into an Immelman - at the top of the climb - <u>disaster struck</u>! We watched in absolute horror as the left wing of his B-47 literally tore off and the plane fell in a crazy corkscrew to earth. A huge fireball erupted when it hit. Capt Shaw was on the radio first - almost screaming as he called the base and told them what happened. The voice on the other end was also upset but rather calm. He said he would dispatch emergency vehicles from the base but must have the exact location of the crash. I studied my chart and scanned the terrain - then I got on the radio and said "The crash site is about 25 miles northeast of Garden City, Kansas - near the intersection of State Highway 136 and U.S. Highway 60. They can't miss it, there is a large fire and a huge column of smoke. The tower responded "Roger - we're on our way."

We were numb - Captain Martinez was a friend and all three of the crew lived within a block of me. Gene and Captain Shaw were talking on the radio and I heard Captain Shaw say "I'm going to abort this mission." Gene came on the intercom and said "Ready boys - it's our turn" Jim argued with him but Gene was set on making the run - he claimed Martinez had snap rolled too hard - that he knew how to do it using a lazy roll out. Jim said "What the heck - you can't live forever - let's go." Gene said "Tommy - you ready." I said - "Why not" and Gene dove earthward - we skimmed across the wheat fields and Gene pulled her up in the immelman maneuver at the top he yelled "bomb away" as I hit the bomb release - the G force terrific - but Gene rolled the B-47 over and eased her back into straight and level - going in the opposite direction. The B-47 had shuddered and we heard strange sounds from her - but we seemed no worse for wear. Gene said "Wow - that was exhilarating - I love it." Jim said "Scary too - let's go home." We climbed back to 20,000 ft and headed east. I looked back at the crash site and the fire had turned a while color. (I later learned it was the magnesium in the metal). There was no doubt that Gene was an excellent pilot - but I questioned his judgment after that stunt.

After we landed and taxied back to the squadron parking area there was a crowd waiting for us. We parked and climbed out of the B-47. Both Colonel Low and Colonel Hempleman met us. I couldn't help but notice that J-P4 fuel was pouring out of the fuselage - right behind the bomb bay. Colonel Low said "Lieutenant Rosselot, I don't know whether to compliment you or chew you're but out - that was a stupid thing to do."

We stood there and listened to the two Colonels for a couple of minutes then Colonel Low said "Let's go to your office and talk." As we walked toward squadron head quarters they had hooked a tractor to our B-47 and were towing it to the hanger - fire trucks were trailing along behind as were about a dozen factory reps and maintenance personnel.

When we got to headquarters, I went to the nearest telephone and called Caro - she was hysterical. She had heard on the radio that a B-47 was down and had no way of knowing if it was us. I finally got her settled down when I said "That made up my mind - I'm getting out."

We went into Colonel Hemp leman's office and were soon joined by the head of maintenance, two factory reps, the Chaplin, and Captain Shaw and his crew. The first thing they grilled us about was Captain Martinez's run and crash. Gene maintained that Martinez had snap rolled too hard - Shaw disagreed and they argued. It was obvious that Shaw was mad as heck at Gene - he felt he had made him look like a coward. While they argued the phone rang - it was for one of the reps. He told us that a fuel line had broken in our B-47 and they had found stress fractures in the "Milk bottle" joints which held the wings on. They also had found cracks in several other fasteners. He said "This brave crew has provided invaluable information - it will probably save many lives." Colonel Low said "That's what I meant".

After they had completed grilling us - Captain Hempleman said "You boys take a couple of days off." We started to leave and the Chaplain asked "Lieutenant Thomas, wasn't Captain Martinez a neighbor? I said "Yes Sir, the entire crew were neighbors." Colonel Hempleman put his arm around my shoulder and said "I hate to ask you to do this and say "No" if you aren't up to it - but it might help if you would join the Chaplain and I when we go visit the families of the crew." I said "I'll do it sir - let me shower first and change." He said "By all means."

I cleaned up and put on my uniform and told them I would drive my car. They said they would follow me. I drove first to Captain Martinez house which was diagonally across the street from my house. We parked, got out, and Mrs. Martinez (Teresa) came to the door. When she saw us she screamed and started bawling - she too had heard the radio and knew what had happened. There is nothing you can do or say that helps under those circumstances. She cried on my shoulder some and I tried to comfort her - but couldn't. They had four little children - stair steps from 1 to about 6. The two oldest were crying but the two youngest really didn't know what was going on.

I glanced out the window and saw Caro standing outside our front door - holding Michael. I told Colonel Hempleman I would be right back then crossed the street and held Caro - who by now was also bawling as was Mike. She wanted to go see Teresa but I convinced her to get back in the house and promised we would go later. It was cold. Once I got her under control I explained that I had to go visit the Gardners and Mispagels and would be back in an hour.

I rejoined Colonel Hempleman and Captain Gordon (The Chaplain) and we walked down the street to the Gardners. Mrs. Gardner (Peggy) answered the door and it was a repeat of the scene at the Martinez - except she only had two small children. Then we crossed the street to the Mispagels and Mrs. Mispagel (Nancy) was a little more composed - but not much. They were relative newlyweds - having been married about six months. I think that was the toughest day of my life. My heart really went out to those young widows and their small children. (And of course - you couldn't help but think - there, but for the grace of God, go I?)

When I returned home, Caro and Michael both were asleep. I decided not to wake them. I got on the phone and called the New York office of the accounting firm and told them I would return to work the first of January. I explained that I did not wish to return to Cincinnati and would prefer the west coast - specifically Oregon or Washington. They said they would check for openings and would call back. In less than an hour, the phone rang. The partner in charge of the Portland, Oregon office was calling and we talked awhile and agreed I would transfer to his office and report on or before January 2nd.

The next couple of days, Caro and I did all we could for the young widows and children - then the funerals were held - more sadness. After all the grieving and sadness - I was ready to return to work.

The next few weeks passed rapidly - we continued to fly and check off our SAC requirements. I broke the news to Gene and Jim that I was getting out - and things were never the same after that. Thanksgiving came - then Christmas. During Christmas Caro was out of sorts again. She finally told me what the problem was. She was homesick and wanted to return to Texas. I finally gave up on my dream of going to the pacific northwest and called the Firm's New York office again. I knew they thought I was crazy and I was fearful they might just fire me when I told them I wanted to go to Texas instead of Oregon. However, the partner I was talking to was a Texan and he thought I was making a wise decision. He said he knew the Dallas office - could use me and would want me. He asked that I stay close to the phone.

Sure enough, within ten minutes the phone rang and it was the Dallas managing partner. He sounded as if he really wanted me so we agreed I would report January 2nd. (I later found out that accountants were in short supply - particularly in booming Dallas).

When I told Caro we were going to Dallas - she cried again. But this time, they were tears of joy. The day after Christmas the movers came by and loaded our possessions. That afternoon, I took Caro and Michael to some friends (Stewart and Martha) and left them and then headed - to a new career and to Texas! (Caro and Michael would fly down in two days).

That dear reader, is my experience in the "Cold War", by far the most expensive war that was never fought. I suppose we won that war. The U.S.S.R. is now fragmented and bankrupt - and we're still intact and afloat. The End.

BOOKS WRITTEN BY
BILL R. THOMAS

Title	Brief Description
1) A Summer on Piney Creek	A Summer Spent with Friend Living in a Cave on Piney Creek (Kentucky)
2) Hickory Fired Tobacco, Moonshine Whiskey, Beautiful Horses, and Fast Women	Kentucky Based Short Stories
3) Bill T's Texas Bob Tales	Texas Based Short Stories
4) I Smell Smoke	Authors Experience as B-47 Crew Member in Strategic Air Command
5) My Most Memorable Adventures - One Hunting and One Fishing	Hunting Trip in Mexico and Fishing Trip in Alaska
6) The Accumulated Wisdom of the Bugscuffle Domino, Whittle and Spit Club	Philosophy and Wisdom Gained Over a Colorful Lifetime
7) The T-Bone Ranch	Developing a Cattle Ranch in Montague County, Texas
8) A Wild Shot In The Dark	Autobiography - Birth Through Air Force
9) The Debits Are On The Left, The Credits Are By The Window	Autobiography - Air Force to Present

www.ingramcontent.com/pod-product-compliance
Lightning Source LLC
Chambersburg PA
CBHW020004050426
42450CB00005B/297